Illusions

I T WAS A question I heard more than once, after
Jonathan Seagull was published. "What are you
going to write next, Richard? After Jonathan, what?"

I answered then that I didn't have to write anything
next, not a word, and that all my books together said everything that I had asked them to say. Having starved for a
while, the car repossessed and that sort of thing, it was fun
not to have to work to midnights.

Still, every summer or so I took my antique biplane
out into the green-meadow seas of midwest America, flew
passengers for three-dollar rides and began to feel an old
tension again – there was something left to say, and I
hadn't said it.

I do not enjoy writing at all. If I can turn my back on an
idea, out there in the dark, if I can avoid opening the door to
it, I won't even reach for a pencil.

But once in a while there's a great dynamite-burst of flying glass and brick and splinters through the front wall and somebody stalks over the rubble, seizes me by the throat and gently says, "I will not let you go until you set me, in words, on paper." That's how I met *Illusions*.

There in the Midwest, even, I'd lie on my back practicing cloud-vaporizing, and I couldn't get the story out of my mind...what if somebody came along who was really good at this, who could teach me how my world works and how to control it? What if I could meet a super-advanced...what if a Siddhartha or a Jesus came into our time, with power over the illusions of the world because he knew the reality behind them? And what if I could meet him in person, if he were flying a biplane and landed in the same meadow with me? What would he say, what would he be like?

Maybe he wouldn't be like the messiah on the oil-streaked grass-stained pages of my journal, maybe he wouldn't say anything this book says. But then again, the things this one told me: that we magnetize into our lives whatever we hold in our thought, for instance – if that is true, then somehow I have brought myself to this moment for a reason, and so have you. Perhaps it is no coincidence that you're holding this book; perhaps there's something about these adventures that you came here to remember. I choose to think so. And I choose to think my messiah is perched out there on some other dimension, not fiction at all, watching us both, and laughing for the fun of it happening just the way we've planned it to be.

Also by Richard Bach

STRANGER TO THE GROUND

BIPLANE

NOTHING BY CHANCE

JONATHAN LIVINGSTON SEAGULL

A GIFT OF WINGS

THERE'S NO SUCH PLACE AS FAR AWAY

THE BRIDGE ACROSS FOREVER:
A LOVESTORY

ONE

RUNNING FROM SAFETY:
AN ADVENTURE OF THE SPIRIT

OUT OF MY MIND

Illusions
The Adventures of a Reluctant Messiah

by Richard Bach

Delta
Trade Paperbacks

A Delta Book
Published by
Dell Publishing
a division of
Random House, Inc.
1540 Broadway
New York, New York 10036

ISBN: 0-385-31925-8

Reprinted by arrangement with Delacorte Press

Manufactured in the United States of America
Published simultaneously in Canada

February 1998

10   9   8   7   6

BVG

1

1. There was a Master come unto the earth, born in the holy land of Indiana, raised in the mystical hills east of Fort Wayne.

2. The Master learned of this world in the public schools of Indiana, and as he grew, in

his trade as a mechanic
of automobiles.

3. But the Master had learnings
from other lands and other
schools, from other lives that
he had lived. He remembered
these, and remembering became
wise and strong, so that others
saw his strength and came
to him for counsel.

4. The Master believed that he
had power to help himself
and all mankind, and as he
believed so it was for him,
so that others saw his
power and came to him to

be healed of their troubles
and their many diseases.

5. The Master believed that it
is well for any man to
think upon himself as a son
of God, and as he believed,
so it was, and the
shops and garages where he
worked became crowded and
jammed with those who sought
his learning and his touch,
and the streets outside
with those who longed only
that the shadow of his
passing might fall upon them,
and change their lives.

6. It came to pass, because of the crowds, that the several foremen and shop managers bid the Master leave his tools and go his way, for so tightly was he thronged that neither he nor other mechanics had room to work upon the automobiles.

7. So it was that he went into the countryside, and people following began to call him Messiah, and worker of miracles; and as they believed, it was so.

8. If a storm passed as he spoke, not a raindrop touched a listener's head; the last of the multitude heard his words as clearly as the first, no matter lightning nor thunder in the sky about. And always he spoke to them in parables.

9. And he said unto them, "within each of us lies the power of our consent to health and to sickness, to riches and to poverty, to freedom and to slavery. It is we who control these, and not another."

10. A mill-man spoke and said,
"Easy words for you, Master,
for you are guided as we
are not, and need not toil
as we toil. A man has to
work for his living in
this world."

11. The Master answered and said,
"Once there lived a village
of creatures along the bottom
of a great crystal river.

12. "The current of the river
swept silently over them
all— young and old, rich
and poor, good and evil,
the current going its own

way, knowing only its own
crystal self.

13. "Each creature in its own
manner clung tightly to the
twigs and rocks of the river
bottom, for clinging was their
way of life, and resisting
the current what each had
learned from birth.

14. "But one creature said at
last, 'I am tired of clinging.
Though I cannot see it
with my eyes, I trust that
the current knows where it is
going. I shall let go, and
let it take me where it

will. Clinging, I shall die
of boredom.'

15. "The other creatures laughed and
said, 'Fool! Let go, and that
current you worship will throw
you tumbled and smashed
across the rocks, and you
will die quicker than boredom!'

16. "But the one heeded them
not, and taking a breath
did let go, and at once
was tumbled and smashed by
the current across the rocks.

17. "Yet in time, as the creature
refused to cling again, the

current lifted him free from the bottom, and he was bruised and hurt no more.

18. "And the creatures downstream, to whom he was a stranger, cried, 'See a miracle! A creature like ourselves, yet he flies! See the Messiah, come to save us all!'

19. "And the one carried in the current said, 'I am no more Messiah than you. The river delights to lift us free, if only we dare let go. Our true work is this voyage, this adventure.'

20. "But they cried the more, 'Saviour!' all the while clinging to the rocks, and when they looked again he was gone, and they were left alone making legends of a Saviour."

21. And it came to pass when he saw that the multitude thronged him the more day on day, tighter and closer and fiercer than ever they had, when he saw that they pressed him to heal them without rest, and feed them always with his miracles, to learn for them and to live their lives, he went alone that day unto a

hilltop apart, and there he prayed.

22. And he said in his heart, Infinite Radiant Is, if it be thy will, let this cup pass from me, let me lay aside this impossible task. I cannot live the life of one other soul, yet ten thousand cry to me for life. I'm sorry I allowed it all to happen. If it be thy will, let me go back to my engines and my tools and let me live as other men.

23. And a voice spoke to him on the hilltop, a voice neither

male nor female, loud nor
soft, a voice infinitely kind.
And the voice said unto him,
"Not my will, but thine be
done. For what is thy will
is mine for thee. Go thy
way as other men, and
be thou happy on the earth."

24. And hearing, the Master was
glad, and gave thanks, and came
down from the hilltop humming
a little mechanic's song.
And when the throng pressed
him with its woes, beseeching
him to heal for it and learn
for it and feed it nonstop
from his understanding and to

entertain it with his wonders,
he smiled upon the multitude
and said pleasantly unto them,
"I quit."

25. For a moment the multitude
was stricken dumb with
astonishment.

26. And he said unto them,
"If a man told God that he
wanted most of all to help the
suffering world, no matter the
price to himself, and God
answered and told him what he
must do, should the man do
as he is told?"

27. "Of course, Master!" cried the many. "It should be pleasure for him to suffer the tortures of hell itself, should God ask it!"

28. "No matter what those tortures, nor how difficult the task?"

29. "Honor to be hanged, glory to be nailed to a tree and burned, if so be that God has asked," said they.

30. "And what would you do," the Master said unto the multitude, "if God spoke directly to your face and said,

'I COMMAND THAT YOU BE HAPPY IN THE WORLD, AS LONG AS YOU LIVE.' What would you do then?"

31. And the multitude was silent, not a voice, not a sound was heard upon the hillsides, across the valleys where they stood.

32. And the Master said unto the silence, "In the path of our happiness shall we find the learning for which we have chosen this lifetime. So it is that I have learned this day, and

choose to leave you now.
to walk your own path,
as you please."

33. And he went his way
through the crowds and
left them, and he
returned to the everyday
world of men and machines.

2

I T WAS toward the middle of the summer that I met
Donald Shimoda. In four years' flying, I had
never found another pilot in the line of work I do: flying with the
wind from town to town, selling rides in an old biplane, three dollars for ten minutes in the air.

But one day just north of Ferris, Illinois, I looked down from
the cockpit of my Fleet and there was an old Travel Air 4000, gold
and white, landed pretty as you please in the lemon-emerald hay.

Mine's a free life, but it does get lonely, sometimes. I saw the
biplane there, thought about it for a few seconds, and decided it
would be no harm to drop in. Throttle back to idle, a full-rudder
slip, and the Fleet and I fell sideways toward the ground. Wind in
the flying wires, that gentle good sound, the slow *pok-pok* of the old

engine loafing its propeller around. Goggles up to better watch the landing. Cornstalks a green-leaf jungle swishing close below, flicker of a fence and then just-cut hay as far as I could see. Stick and rudder out of the slip, a nice little round-out above the land, hay brushing the tires, then the familiar calm crashing rattle of hard ground under-wheel, slowing, slowing and now a quick burst of noise and power to taxi beside the other plane and stop. Throttle back, switch off, the soft *clack-clack* of the propeller spinning down to stop in the total quiet of July.

The pilot of the Travel Air sat in the hay, his back against the left wheel of his airplane, and he watched me.

For half a minute I watched him, too, looking at the mystery of his calm. I wouldn't have been so cool just to sit there and watch another plane land in a field with me and park ten yards away. I nodded, liking him without knowing why.

"You looked lonely," I said across the distance between us.

"So did you."

"Don't mean to bother you. If I'm one too many, I'll be on my way."

"No. I've been waiting for you."

I smiled at that. "Sorry I'm late."

"That's all right."

I pulled off my helmet and goggles, climbed out of the cockpit and stepped to the ground. This feels good, when you've been a couple hours in the Fleet.

"Hope you don't mind ham and cheese," he said. "Ham and cheese and maybe an ant." No handshake, no introduction of any kind.

26

He was not a large man. Hair to his shoulders, blacker than the rubber of the tire he leaned against. Eyes dark as hawk's eyes, the kind I like in a friend, and in anyone else make me uncomfortable indeed. He could have been a karate master on his way to some quietly violent demonstration.

I accepted the sandwich and a thermos cup of water. "Who are you, anyway?" I said. "Years, I've been hopping rides, never seen another barnstormer out in the fields."

"Not much else I'm fit to do," he said, happily enough. "A little mechanicking, welding, roughneck a bit, skinning Cats; I stay in one place too long, I get problems. So I made the airplane and now I'm in the barnstorming business."

"What kind of Cat?" I've been mad for diesel tractors since I was a kid.

"D-Eights, D-Nines. Just for a little while, in Ohio."

"D-Nines! Big as a house! Double compound low gear, can they really push a mountain?"

"There are better ways of moving mountains," he said with a smile that lasted for maybe a tenth of a second.

I leaned for a minute against the lower wing of his plane, watching him. A trick of the light...it was hard to look at the man closely. As if there were a light around his head, fading the background a faint, misty silver.

"Something wrong?" he asked.

"What kind of problems did you have?"

"Oh, nothing much. I just like to keep moving these days, same as you."

I took my sandwich and walked around his plane. It was a 1928 or 1929 machine, and it was completely unscratched. Factories don't make airplanes as new as his was, parked there in the hay. Twenty coats of hand-rubbed butyrate dope, at least, paint like a mirror pulled tight over the wooden ribs of the thing. *Don,* in old-English gold leaf under the rim of his cockpit, and the registration on the map case said, *D. W. Shimoda.* The instruments were new out of the box, original 1928 flight instruments. Varnished-oak control stick and rudder-bar; throttle, mixture, spark advance at the left. You never see spark advances anymore, even on the best-restored antiques. No scratch anywhere, not a patch on the fabric, not a single streak of engine oil from the cowling. Not a blade of straw on the floor of the cockpit, as though his machine hadn't flown at all, but instead had materialized on the spot through some time-warp across half a century. I felt an odd creepy cold on my neck.

"How long you been hopping passengers?" I called across the plane to him.

"About a month, now, five weeks."

He was lying. Five weeks in the fields and I don't care who you are, you've got dirt and oil on the plane and there's straw on the cockpit floor, no matter what. But this machine...no oil on the windshield, no flying-hay stains on the leading edges of wings and tail, no bugs smashed on the propeller. That is not possible for an airplane flying through an Illinois summer. I studied the Travel Air another five minutes, and then I went back and sat down in the hay under the wing, facing the pilot. I wasn't afraid, I still liked the guy, but something was wrong.

"Why are you not telling me the truth?"

"I have told you the truth, Richard," he said. The name is painted on my airplane, too.

"A person does not hop passengers for a month in a Travel Air without getting a little oil on the plane, my friend, a little dust? One patch in the fabric? Hay, for God's sake, on the floor?"

He smiled calmly at me. "There are some things you do not know."

In that moment he was a strange other-planet person. I believed what he said, but I had no way of explaining his jewel airplane parked out in the summer hayfield.

"This is true. But some day I'll know them all. And then you can have my airplane, Donald, because I won't need it to fly."

He looked at me with interest, and raised his black eyebrows. "Oh? Tell me."

I was delighted. Someone wanted to hear my theory!

"People couldn't fly for a long time, I don't think, because they didn't think it was possible, so of course they didn't learn the first little principle of aerodynamics. I want to believe that there's another principle somewhere: we don't need airplanes to fly, or move through walls, or get to planets. We can learn how to do that without machines anywhere. If we want to."

He half-smiled, seriously, and nodded his head one time. "And you think that you will learn what you wish to learn by hopping three-dollar rides out of hayfields."

"The only learning that's mattered is what I got on my own, doing what I want to do. There isn't, but if there were a soul on earth who could teach me more of what I want to know than my airplane can, and the sky, I'd be off right now to find him. Or her."

The dark eyes looked at me level. "Don't you believe you're guided, if you really want to learn this thing?"

"I'm guided, yes. Isn't everyone? I've always felt something kind of watching over me, sort of."

"And you think you'll be led to a teacher who can help you."

"If the teacher doesn't happen to be me, yes."

"Maybe that's the way it happens," he said.

A modern new pickup truck hushed down the road toward us, raising a thin brown fog of dust, and it stopped by the field. The door opened, an old man got out, and a girl of ten or so. The dust stayed in the air, it was that still.

"Selling rides, are you?" said the man.

The field was Donald Shimoda's discovery; I stayed quiet.

"Yes, sir," he said brightly. "Feel like flyin', do you today?"

"If I did, you cut any didoes, turn any flip-flops with me up there?" The man's eyes twinkled, watching to see if we knew him behind his country-bumpkin talk.

"Will if you want, won't if you don't."

"And you want the dear Lord's fortune, I suppose."

"Three dollars cash, sir, for nine, ten minutes in the air. That is thirty-three and one-third cents per minute. And worth it, most people tell me."

It was an odd bystander-feeling, to sit there idle and listen to the way this fellow worked his trade. I liked what he said, all low key. I had grown so used to my own way of selling rides ("*Guaran-*

teed ten degrees cooler upstairs, folks! Come on up where only birds and angels fly! All of this for three dollars only, a dozen quarters from your purse or pocket . . ."), I had forgotten there might be another.

There's a tension, flying and selling rides alone. I was used to it, but still it was there: if I don't fly passengers, I don't eat. Now when I could sit back, not depending for my dinner on the outcome, I relaxed for once and watched.

The girl stood back and watched, too. Blonde, brown-eyed, solemn-faced, she was here because her grampa was. She did not want to fly.

Most often it's the other way around, eager kids and cautious elders, but one gets a sense for these things when it's one's livelihood, and I knew that girl wouldn't fly with us if we waited all summer.

"Which one of you gentlemen . . . ?" the man said.

Shimoda poured himself a cup of water. "Richard will fly you. I'm still on my lunch hour. Unless you want to wait."

"No, sir, I'm ready to go. Can we fly over my farm?"

"Sure," I said. "Just point the way you want to go, sir." I dumped my bedroll and toolbag and cook pots from the front cockpit of the Fleet, helped the man into the passenger seat and buckled him in. Then I slid down into the rear cockpit and fastened my own seat belt.

"Give me a prop, will you, Don?"

"Yep." He brought his water cup with him and stood by the propeller. "What do you want?"

"Hot and brakes. Pull it slow. The impulse will take it right out of your hand."

31

Always when somebody pulls the Fleet propeller, they pull it too fast, and for complicated reasons the engine won't start. But this man pulled it around ever so slowly, as though he had done it forever. The impulse spring snapped, sparks fired in the cylinders and the old engine was running, that easy. He walked back to his airplane, sat down and began talking to the girl.

In a great burst of raw horsepower and flying straw the Fleet was in the air, climbing through a hundred feet (if the engine quits now, we land in the corn), five hundred feet (now, and we can turn back and land in the hay... now, and it's the cow pasture west), eight hundred feet and level, following the man's finger pointing through the wind southwest.

Three minutes airborne and we circled a farmstead, barns the color of glowing coals, house of ivory in a sea of mint. A garden in back for food: sweet-corn and lettuce and tomatoes growing.

The man in the front cockpit looked down through the air as we circled the farmhouse framed between the wings and through the flying wires of the Fleet.

A woman appeared on the porch below, white apron over blue dress, waving. The man waved back. They would talk later of how they could see each other so well across the sky.

He looked back at me finally with a nod to say that was enough, thanks, and we could head back now.

I flew a wide circle around Ferris, to let the people know there was flying going on, and spiraled down over the hayfield to show them just where it was happening. As I slipped down to land, banked steeply over the corn, the Travel Air swept off the ground and turned at once toward the farm we had just left.

I flew once with a five-ship circus, and for a moment it was that kind of busy feeling...one plane lifting off with passengers while another lands. We touched the ground with a gentle rumbling crash and rolled to the far end of the hay, by the road.

The engine stopped, the man unsnapped his safety belt and I helped him out. He took a wallet from his overalls and counted the dollar bills, shaking his head.

"That's quite a ride, son."

"We think so. It's a good product we're selling."

"It's your friend, that's selling!"

"Oh?"

"I'll say. Your friend could sell ashes to the devil, I'll wager, can't he now?"

"How come you say that?"

"The girl, of course. An airplane ride to my granddaughter, Sarah!" As he spoke he watched the Travel Air, a distant silver mote in the air, circling the farmhouse. He spoke as a calm man speaks, noting the dead twig in the yard has just sprouted blossoms and ripe apples.

"Since she's born, that girl's been wild to death about high places. Screams. Just terrified. Sarah'd no more climb a tree than she'd stir hornets barehand. Won't climb the ladder to the loft, won't go up there if the Flood was rising in the yard. The girl's a wonder with machines, not too bad around animals, but heights, they are a caution to her! And there she is up in the air."

He talked on about this and other special times; he remembered when the barnstormers used to come through Galesburg, years ago, and Monmouth, flying two-wingers the same as we

33

flew, but doing all kinds of crazy stunts with them.

I watched the distant Travel Air get bigger, spiral down over the field in a bank steeper than I'd ever fly with a girl afraid of heights, slip over the corn and the fence and touch the hay in a three-point landing that was dazzling to watch. Donald Shimoda must have been flying for a good long while, to land a Travel Air that way.

The airplane rolled to a stop beside us, no extra power required and the propeller clanked softly to stop. I looked closely. There were no bugs on the propeller. Not so much as a single fly killed on that eight-foot blade.

I sprang to help, unshackled the girl's safety belt, opened the little front-cockpit door for her and showed her where to step so her foot wouldn't go through the wing fabric.

"How'd you like that?" I said.

She didn't know I spoke.

"Grampa, I'm not afraid! I wasn't scared, honest! The house looked like a little *toy* and Mom waved at me and Don said I was scared just because I fell and died once and I don't have to be afraid anymore! I'm going to be a pilot, Grampa. I'm gonna have an airplane and work on the engine myself and fly everywhere and give rides! Can I do that?"

Shimoda smiled at the man and shrugged his shoulders.

"He told you you were going to be a pilot, did he, Sarah?"

"No, but I am. I'm already good with engines, you know that!"

"Well, you can talk about that with your mother. Time for us to be getting home."

The two thanked us and one walked, one ran to the pickup

truck, both changed by what had happened in the field and in the sky.

Two automobiles arrived, then another, and we had a noon rush of people who wanted to see Ferris from the air. We flew twelve or thirteen flights as fast as we could get them off, and after that I made a run to the station in town to get car gas for the Fleet. Then a few passengers, a few more, and it was evening and we flew solid back-to-back flights till sunset.

A sign somewhere said *Population 200,* and by dark I was thinking we had flown them all, and some out-of-towners as well.

I forgot in the rush of flying to ask about Sarah and what Don had told her, whether he had made up the story or if he thought it was true, about dying. And every once in a while I watched his plane closely while passengers changed seats. Not a mark on it, no oil-drop anywhere, and he apparently flew to dodge the bugs that I had to wipe from my windshield every hour or two.

There was just a little light in the sky when we quit. By the time I laid dry cornstalks in my tin stove, set them over with charcoal bricks and lit the fire, it was full dark, the firelight throwing colors back from the airplanes parked close, and from the golden straw about us.

I peered into the grocery box. "It's soup or stew or Spaghetti-O's," I said. "Or pears or peaches. Want some hot peaches?"

"No difference," he said mildly. "Anything or nothing."

"Man, aren't you hungry? This has been a busy day!"

"You haven't given me much to be hungry for, unless that's good stew."

I opened the stew can with my Swiss Air Officer's Escape and

Evasion Knife, did a similar job on the Spaghetti-O's, and popped both cans over the fire.

My pockets were tight with cash... this was one of the pleasanter times of day for me. I pulled the bills out and counted, not bothering much to fold them flat. It came to $147, and I figured in my head, which is not easy for me.

"That's...that's...let's see...four and carry the two... forty-nine flights today! Broke a hundred-dollar day, Don, just me and the Fleet! You must have broke two hundred easy...you fly mostly two at a time?"

"Mostly," he said.

"About this teacher you're looking for..." he said.

"I ain't lookin' for no teacher," I said. "I am counting *money*! I can go a *week* on this, I can be rained out cold for one solid week!"

He looked at me and smiled. "When you are done swimming in your money," he said, "would you mind passing my stew?"

3

THRONGS and masses and crowds of people, torrents of humanity pouring against one man in the middle of them all. Then the people became an ocean that would drown the man, but instead of drowning he walked over the ocean, whistling, and disappeared. The ocean of water changed to an ocean of grass. A white-and-gold Travel Air 4000 came down to land on the grass and the pilot got out of the cockpit and put up a cloth sign: FLY – $3 – FLY.

It was three o'clock in the morning when I woke from the dream, remembering it all and for some reason happy for it. I opened my eyes to see in the moonlight that big Travel Air parked alongside the Fleet. Shimoda sat on his bedroll as he had when first I met him, leaning back against the left wheel of his airplane. It wasn't that I saw him clearly, I just knew he was there.

"Hi, Richard," he said quietly in the dark. "Does that tell you what's going on?"

"Does what tell me?" I said foggily. I was still remembering and didn't think to be surprised that he'd be awake.

"Your dream. The guy and the crowds and the airplane," he said patiently. "You were curious about me, so now you know, OK? There were news stories: Donald Shimoda, the one they were beginning to call the Mechanic Messiah, the American Avatar, who disappeared one day in front of twenty-five thousand eyewitnesses?"

I did remember that, had read it on a small-town Ohio newspaper rack, because it was on the front page.

"Donald Shimoda?"

"At your service," he said. "Now you know, so you don't have to puzzle me out anymore. Go back to sleep."

I thought about that for a long time before I slept.

"Are you allowed...I didn't think...you get a job like that, the Messiah, you're supposed to save the world, aren't you? I didn't know the Messiah could just turn in his keys like that and quit." I sat high on the top cowling of the Fleet and considered my strange friend. "Toss me a nine-sixteenths, would you please, Don?"

He hunted in the toolbag and pitched the wrench up to me. As with the other tools that morning, the one he threw slowed and stopped within a foot of me, floating weightless, turning lazy in midair. The moment I touched it, though, it went heavy in my hand, an everyday chrome-vanadium aircraft end-wrench. Well, not quite everyday. Ever since a cheap seven-eighths broke in my hand I've bought the best tools a man can have...this one happened to be a Snap-On, which as any mechanic knows is not your everyday wrench. Might as well be made of gold, the price of the thing, but it's a joy in the hand and you know it will never break, no matter what you do with it.

"Of course you can quit! Quit anything you want, if you change your mind about doing it. You can quit breathing, if you want to." He floated a Phillips screwdriver for his own amusement. "So I quit being the Messiah, and if I sound a little defensive, it's maybe because I am still a little defensive. Better that than keeping the job and hating it. A good messiah hates nothing and is free to walk any path he wants to walk. Well, that's true for everybody, of course. We're all the sons of God, or children of the Is, or ideas of the Mind, or however else you want to say it."

I worked at tightening the cylinder-base nuts on the Kinner engine. A good powerplant, the old B-5, but these nuts want to loosen themselves every hundred flying hours or so, and it's wise to stay one jump ahead. Sure enough, the first one I put the wrench to went a quarter-turn tighter, and I was glad for my wisdom to check them all this morning, before flying any more customers.

"Well, yes, Don, but it seems as if Messiahing would be different from other jobs, you know? Jesus going back to hammering nails for a living? Maybe it just sounds odd."

He considered that, trying to see my point. "I don't see your point. Strange thing about that is he didn't quit when they first started calling him Saviour. Instead of leaving at that piece of bad news, he tried logic: 'OK, I'm the son of God, but so are we all; I'm the saviour, but so are you! The works that I do, you can do!' Anybody in their right mind understands that."

39

It was hot, up on the cowling, but it didn't feel like work. The more I want to get something done, the less I call it work. Satisfying, to know that I was keeping the cylinders from flying off the engine.

"Say you want another wrench," he said.

"I do not want another wrench. And I happen to be so spiritually advanced that I consider these tricks of yours mere party games, Shimoda, of a moderately evolved soul. Or maybe a beginning hypnotist."

"A hypnotist! Boy, are you ever getting warm! But better hypnotist than Messiah. What a dull job! Why didn't I know it was going to be a dull job?"

"You did," I said wisely. He just laughed.

"Did you ever consider, Don, that it might not be so easy to quit, after all? That you might not just settle right down to the life of a normal human being?"

He didn't laugh at that. "You're right, of course," he said, and ran his fingers through his black hair. "Stay in any one place too long, more than a day or two, and people knew I was something strange. Brush against my sleeve, you're healed of terminal cancer, and before the week's out there I'm back in the middle of a crowd again. This airplane keeps me moving, and nobody knows where I came from or where I'm going next, which suits me pretty well."

"You are gonna have a tougher time than you think, Don."
"Oh?"

"Yeah, the whole motion of our time is from the material toward the spiritual...slow as it is, it's still a pretty huge motion. I don't think the world is gonna let you alone."

"It's not me they want, it's the miracles! And those I can teach to somebody else; let him be the Messiah. I won't tell him it's a dull job. And besides, *'There is no problem so big that it cannot be run away from.'* "

I slid from the cowling down to the hay and began tightening the cylinder nuts on number three and four cylinders. Not all of them were loose, but some were. "You are quoting Snoopy the Dog, I believe?"

"I'll quote the truth wherever I find it, thank you."

"You can't run away, Don! What if I start worshiping you right now? What if I get tired of working on my engine and start begging you to heal it for me? Look, I'll give you every dime I make from now to sundown if you just teach me how to float in the air! If you don't do it, then I'll know that I'm supposed to start praying to you, Holy One Sent to Lift My Burden."

He just smiled at me. I still don't think he understood that he couldn't run away. How could I know that when he didn't?

"Did you have the whole show, like you see in the movies from India? Crowds in the streets, billions of hands touching you, flowers and incense, golden platforms with silver tapestries for you to stand on when you spoke?"

"No. Even before I asked for the job, I knew I couldn't stand that. So I chose the United States, and I just got the crowds."

It was pain for him, remembering, and I was sorry I had brought the whole thing up.

He sat in the hay and talked on, looking through me. "I wanted to say, for the love of God, if you want freedom and joy so much, can't you see it's not anywhere outside of you? Say you have it, and you have it! Act as if it's yours, and it is! Richard, what is so damned hard about that? But they didn't even hear, most of

41

them. Miracles – like going to auto races to see the crashes, they came to me to see miracles. First it's frustrating and then after a while it just gets dull. I have no idea how the other messiahs could stand it."

"You put it that way, it does lose some of its charm," I said. I tightened the last nut and put the tools away. "Where are we headed today?"

He walked to my cockpit, and instead of wiping the bugs off my windshield, he passed his hand over it and the smashed little creatures came alive and flew away. His own windshield never needed cleaning, of course, and now I knew his engine would never need any maintenance, either.

"I don't know," he said. "I don't know where we're headed."

"What do you mean? You know the past and the future of all things. You know exactly where we're going!"

He sighed. "Yeah. But I try not to think about it."

For a while, as I was working on the cylinders, I got to thinking wow, all I have to do is stay with this guy and there will be no problems, nothing bad will happen and everything will turn out fine. But the way he said that: "I try not to think about it," made me remember what had happened to the other Messiahs sent into this world. Common sense shouted at me to turn south after takeoff and get as far away from the man as I could get. But as I said, it gets lonely, flying this way alone, and I was glad to find him, just to have somebody to talk with who knew an aileron from a vertical stabilizer.

I should have turned south, but after takeoff I stayed with him and we flew north and east into that future that he tried not to think about.

4

Where do you learn all this stuff, Don? You know so much, or maybe I just think you do. No. You do know a lot. Is it all practice? Don't you get any formal training to be a Master?"

"They give you a book to read."

I hung a fresh-washed silk scarf on the flying wires and stared at him. "A book?"

"*Saviour's Manual.* It's kind of the bible for masters. There's a copy around here somewhere, if you're interested."

"Yes, yes! You mean a regular book that tells you...?"

He rummaged around for a while in the baggage space behind the headrest of the Travel Air and came up with a small volume bound in what looked like suede.

Messiah's Handbook,
&
Reminders for the Advanced Soul.

"What do you mean, *Saviour's Manual*? This says *Messiah's Handbook.*"

"Something like that." He started to pick up things around his airplane, as though he thought it was time to be moving on.

I leafed through the book, a collection of maxims and short paragraphs.

Perspective –
Use It or Lose It.
If you turned to this page,
you're forgetting that what is going
on around you is not reality.
Think about that.
Remember where you came from,
where you're going, and why you created
the mess you got yourself into in the first place.
You're going to die a horrible death, remember.
It's all good training, and you'll enjoy it
more if you keep the facts
in mind.

*Take your dying with some seriousness, however.
Laughing on the way to your execution
is not generally understood by less-
advanced life-forms, and they'll
call you crazy.*

"Have you read this, about losing your perspective, Don?"
"No."
"It says you have to die a horrible death."

45

"You don't have to. Depends on the circumstances, and how you feel like arranging things."

"Are you going to die a horrible death?"

"I don't know. Not much point in it, would you think, now that I've quit the job? A quiet little ascension ought to be enough. I'll decide in a few weeks, when I finish what I came for."

I put him down for kidding, the way he did from time to time, and didn't know then that he was serious about the few weeks.

I went on into the book; it was the kind of knowledge a master would need, all right.

Learning
is finding out
what you already know.
Doing is demonstrating that
you know it.
Teaching is reminding others
that they know just as well as you.

You are all learners,
doers, teachers.

Your only
obligation in any lifetime
is to be true to yourself.
Being true to anyone else or
anything else is not only
impossible, but the
mark of a fake
messiah.

The
simplest questions
are the most profound.
Where were you born? Where is your home?
Where are you going? What are you doing?
Think about
these once in a while, and
watch your answers
change.

Y*ou*
teach best
what you most need
to learn.

"You're awfully quiet over there, Richard," said Shimoda, as though he wanted to talk with me.

"Yeah," I said, and went on reading. If this was a book for masters only, I didn't want to let go of it.

L*ive*
never to be
ashamed if anything you do
or say is published
around the world –
even if
what is published
is not true.

Your friends
will know you better
in the first minute you meet
than
  your acquaintances
  will know you in
    a thousand
      years.

The
best way
  to avoid responsibility
is to say, "I've got
responsibilities."

I noticed something strange about the book. "The pages don't have numbers on them, Don."

49

"No," he said. "You just open it and whatever you need most is there."

"A magic book!"

"No. You can do it with any book. You can do it with an old newspaper, if you read carefully enough. Haven't you done that, hold some problem in your mind, then open any book handy and see what it tells you?"

"No."

"Well, try it sometime."

I tried. I closed my eyes and wondered what was going to happen to me if I stayed much longer with this strange person. It was fun to be with him, but I couldn't shake the sense that something not fun at all was going to happen to him before long, and I didn't want to be around when it did. Thinking that, I opened the book with my eyes still closed, then opened them and read.

You are led
through your lifetime
by the inner learning creature,
the playful spiritual being
that is your real self. Don't turn away
from possible futures
before you're certain you don't have
anything to learn from them.

You're always free
to change your mind and
choose a different future, or
a different
past.

Choose a different past? Literally or figuratively or how did it mean...?"I think my mind just boggled, Don. I don't know how I could possibly learn this stuff."

"Practice. A little theory and a lot of practice," he said. "Take you about a week and a half."

"A week and a half."

"Yeah. Believe you know all answers, and you know all answers. Believe you're a master, and you are."

"I never said I wanted to be any master."

"That's right," he said. "You didn't."

But I kept the handbook, and he never asked for it back.

5

FARMERS in the Midwest need good land for their work to prosper. So do gypsy fliers. They have to be close to their customers. They must find fields a block from town, fields planted in grass, or hay or oats or wheat cut grass-short; no cows nearby to eat the fabric from their planes; alongside a road for cars; a gate in the fence for people; fields lined so that an airplane doesn't have to fly low over any house anywhere; smooth enough their machines aren't jolted to pieces rolling 50 mph over the ground; long enough to get in and out safely in the hot calm days of summer; and permission from the owner to fly there for a day.

I thought of this as we flew north through Saturday morning, the messiah and me, the green and gold of the land pulling softly by, a thousand feet below. Donald Shimoda's Travel Air floated noisily off my right wing, bouncing sunlight all directions off its mirror paints. A lovely airplane, I thought, but too big for real hard-times barnstorming. It does carry two passengers at a time, but it also weighs twice as much as a Fleet, and so needs much more field to get off the ground and back on. I owned a Travel Air once, but traded it finally for the Fleet, which can get into tiny fields, fields the size you're a lot more likely to find close to town. I could work a 500-foot field with the Fleet, where the Travel Air took 1000, 1300 feet. You tie yourself to this guy, I thought, and you tie yourself to the limits of his airplane.

And sure enough, the moment I thought that, I spotted a neat little cow pasture by the town going past below. It was a standard 1320-foot farm-field cut in half the other half sold to the town for a baseball diamond.

Knowing Shimoda's plane couldn't land there, I kicked my little flying machine up on her left wing, nose up, power to idle, and sank like a safe toward the ball park. We touched in the grass just beyond the left-field fence and rolled to a stop with room to spare. I just wanted to show off a little, show him what a Fleet can do, properly flown.

A burst of throttle swung me around for takeoff again, but when I turned to go, there was the Travel Air all set up on final approach to land. Tail down, right wing up, it looked like some glorious graceful condor turning to land on a broom-straw.

He was low and slow, so that the hair on my neck prickled. I was about to see a crash. A Travel Air, you want to hold at least 60 mph over the fence to land, slower than that with an airplane that stalls at 50 and you are going to wrap it up in a ball. But what I saw was this gold and snow biplane stop in the air, instead. Well, I don't mean stop, but it was flying no more than 30 mph, an airplane that stalls at 50, mind you, stop in the air and sort of sigh three-point onto the grass. He used half, maybe three-quarters the space I had used to land the Fleet.

I just sat in the cockpit and looked, while he taxied alongside and shut down. When I turned off my engine, still staring at him dumbly, he called "Nice field, you found! Close enough to town, hey?"

Our first customers, two boys on a Honda motorcycle, were already turning in to see what was going on.

"What do you mean, close to town?" I shouted over the engine noise still in my ears.

"Well, it's half a block away!"

"No, not that! WHAT WAS THAT LANDING? In the Travel Air! How did you land here?"

He winked at me. "Magic!"

"No, Don... really! I saw the way you landed!"

He could see that I was shocked and more than a bit frightened.

"Richard, do you want to know the answer to floating wrenches in the air and healing all sickness and turning water into wine and walking on the waves and landing Travel Airs on a hundred feet of grass? Do you want to know the answer to all these miracles?"

I felt as though he had turned a laser on me. "I want to know how you landed here..."

"Listen!" he called across the gulf between us. "This world? And everything in it? *Illusions*, Richard! Every bit of it *illusions! Do you understand that?"* There was no wink, no smile; as though he was suddenly furious with me for not knowing long ago.

The motorcycle stopped by the tail of his airplane; the boys looked eager to fly.

"Yeah," was all I could think to say. "Roger on the illusions." Then they were on him for a ride and it was up to me to find the owner of the field before he found us and ask permission to fly out of his cow pasture.

The only way to describe the takeoffs and landings the Travel Air made that day is to tell you that it looked like a fake Travel Air. As if the plane were really an E-2 Cub, or a helicopter dressed in a Travel Air costume. Somehow it was a lot easier for me to accept a nine-sixteenths end-wrench floating weightless than to be calm watching that airplane of his lift off the ground with passengers aboard at 30 mph. It is one thing to believe in levitation when you see it, it is another thing entirely to believe in miracles.

I kept thinking about what he had said so fiercely. Illusions. Someone had said that before . . . when I was a kid, learning magic – *magicians* say that! They carefully tell us, "Look, this is not a miracle you are about to see; this is not really magic. What it is, is an effect, it is the illusion of magic." Then they pull a chandelier from a walnut and change an elephant into a tennis racket.

In a burst of insight, I pulled the *Messiah's Handbook* from my pocket and opened it. Two sentences stood alone on the page.

*There is
no such thing as a problem
without a gift for you
in its hands.
You seek problems
because you need
their gifts.*

I didn't quite know why, but reading that eased my confusions. I read it over until I knew it with my eyes closed.

The name of the town was Troy, and the pasture there promised to be as good to us as the hayfield in Ferris had been. But in Ferris I had felt a certain calm, and here was a tension in the air that I didn't like at all.

The flying that was a once-in-a-lifetime adventure to our passengers was for me routine, overshadowed by that strange uneasiness. My adventure was this character I was flying with...the impossible way he made his airplane go and the odd things that he had said to explain it.

The people of Troy were no more stunned by the miracle of the Travel Air's flight than I would have been had some town bell rung at noon that hadn't rung for sixty years...they didn't know that it was impossible for what was happening to happen.

"Thanks for the ride!" they said, and, "Is this all you do for a living...don't you work somewhere?" and, "Why'd you pick a little place like Troy?" and, "Jerry your farm's no bigger than a shoebox!"

We had a busy afternoon. There were lots of people coming out to fly and we were going to make a lot of money. Still, part of me began to say get out get out, get away from this place. I have ignored that before, and always been sorry for it.

About three o'clock I had shut down my engine for gas, walked twice back and forth from the Skelly station with two five-gallon cans of car gas, when it struck me that not once had I seen the Travel Air refuel. Shimoda hadn't put gas in his plane since sometime before Ferris, and I had watched him fly that machine for seven hours now, going on eight, without another drop of gas or oil. And though I knew that he was a good man, and wouldn't hurt me, I was frightened again. If you really stretch it, throttle back to minimum revolutions and mixture dead lean in cruise, you can make a Travel Air run five hours at the outside. But not eight hours of takeoffs and landings.

He flew steadily on, ride after ride, while I poured the Regular into my center-section tank and added a quart of oil to the engine. There was a line of people waiting to fly. . . it was as if he didn't want to disappoint them.

I caught him, though, as he helpéd a man and wife into the front cockpit of his plane. I tried to sound just as calm and casual as I could.

"Don, how you doin' on fuel? Need any gas?" I stood at his wingtip with an empty five-gallon can in my hand.

He looked straight into my eyes and he frowned, puzzled, as though I had asked if he needed any air to breathe.

"No," he said, and I felt like a slow first-grader at the back of the classroom. "No, Richard, I don't need any gas."

It annoyed me. I know a little bit about airplane engines and fuel. "Well then," I flared at him, "how about some uranium?"

He laughed and melted me at once. "No thanks. I filled it last year." And then he was in his cockpit and gone with his passengers in that supernatural slow-motion takeoff.

I wished first that the people would go home, then that we would get out of here fast, people or not, then that I would have the sense to get out of there alone, at once. All I wanted was to take off and find a big empty field far away from any town and just sit and think and write what was happening in my journal, make some sense out of it.

I stayed out of the Fleet, resting till Shimoda landed again. I walked to his cockpit, there in the propeller-blast of the big engine.

"I've flown about enough, Don. Gonna be on my way, land out from towns and be a little less busy for a while. It's been fun flying with you. See you again sometime, OK?"

He didn't blink. "One more flight and I'll be with you. Guy's been waiting."

"All right."

The guy was waiting in a battered wheelchair rolled down the block to the field. He was kind of smashed down and twisted into the seat as if by some high-gravity force, but he was here because he wanted to go flying. There were other people around, forty or fifty, some in, some out of their cars, watching curiously how Don would get the man from the chair into the plane.

He didn't think about it at all. "Do you want to fly?" The man in the wheelchair smiled a twisted smile and nodded sideways.

"Let's go, let's do it!" Don said quietly, as though he was talking to someone who had waited on the sidelines a long while, whose time had come to go into the game again. If there was anything strange about that moment, looking back on it, it was the intensity with which he spoke. It was casual, yes, but it was a command, too, that expected the man to get up and get into the plane, no excuses. What happened then, it was as if the man had been acting, and finished the last scene of his crippled-invalid part. It looked staged. The high-gravity broke away from him as though it was never there; he launched off the chair at a half-run, amazed at himself, toward the Travel Air.

I was standing close, and heard him. "What did you do?" he said. *"What did you do to me?"*

"Are you going to fly or not going to fly?" Don said. "The price is three dollars. Pay me before takeoff, please."

"I'm flying!" he said. Shimoda didn't help him into the front cockpit, the way he usually helped his passengers.

The people in the cars were out of the cars – there was an odd murmur from the watchers and then shocked silence. The man hadn't walked since his truck went off a bridge eleven years before.

Like a kid putting on bedsheet wings, he hopped to the cockpit and slid down into the seat, moving his arms a lot as though he had just been given arms to play with.

Before anybody could talk, Don pressed the throttle and the Travel Air rolled up into the air, steep-turning around the trees and climbing like fury.

Can a moment be happy and at the same time terrifying? There followed a lot of moments like that. It was wonder at what could only be called a miraculous healing to a man who looked like he deserved it, and at the same time, something uncomfortable was going to happen when those two came down again. The crowd was a tight knot waiting, and a tight knot of people is a mob and that is not good at all. Minutes ticked, eyes bored into that little biplane flying so carefree in the sun, and some violent thing was set to go off.

The Travel Air flew some steep lazy eights, a tight spiral, and

61

then it was floating over the fence like a slow noisy flying saucer to land. If he had any sense at all, he would let his passenger off at the far side of the field, take off fast and disappear. There were more people coming; another wheelchair, pushed by a lady running.

He taxied toward the crowd, spun the plane about to keep the propeller pointing away, shut down the engine. The people ran to the cockpit, and for a minute I thought they were going to tear fabric from the fuselage, to get at the two.

Was it cowardly? I don't know. I walked to my airplane, pumped the throttle and primer, pulled the propeller to start the engine. Then I got into the cockpit and turned the Fleet into the wind and took off. The last I saw of Donald Shimoda, he was sitting on the rim of his cockpit, and the mob had him surrounded.

I turned east, then southeast, and after a while the first big field I found with trees for shade and a stream to drink from, I landed for the night. It was a long way from any town.

6

To THIS day I can't say what it was came over me. It was just that doom feeling, and it drove me out, away even from the strange curious fellow that was Donald Shimoda. If I have to fraternize with doom, even the Messiah Himself is not powerful enough to make me hang around.

It was quiet in the field, a silent huge meadow open to the sky...the only sound a little stream I had to listen pretty hard to hear. Lonely again. A person gets used to being alone, but break it just for a day and you have to get used to it again, all over from the beginning.

"OK, so it was fun for a while," I said aloud to the meadow. "It was fun and maybe I had a lot to learn from the guy. But I get enough of crowds even when they're happy...if they're scared they're either going to crucify somebody or worship him. I'm sorry, that's too much!"

Saying that caught me short. The words I had said could have been Shimoda's exactly. Why did he stay there? I had the sense to leave, and I was no messiah at all.

Illusions. What did he mean about illusions? That mattered more than anything he had said or done – fierce, he was, when he said, *"It's all illusions!"* as though he could blast the idea into my head with sheer force. It was a problem, all right, and I needed its gift, but I still didn't know what it meant.

I got a fire going after a while, cooked me up a kind of leftover goulash of bits and pieces of soybean meat and dry noodles and two hot dogs from three days ago that boiling should have been good for. The toolbag was crushed alongside the grocery box, and for no reason I fetched out the nine-sixteenths and looked at it, wiped it clean and stirred the goulash with it.

I was alone, mind you, no one to watch, so for fun I tried floating it in the air, the way he had done it. If I tossed it right straight up and blinked my eyes when it stopped going up and started coming down, I got a half-second feeling that it was floating. But then it thunked back down on the grass or on my knee and the effect was shattered fast. But this very same wrench...How did he do it?

If that's all illusion, Mister Shimoda, then what is it that is real? And if this life is illusion, why do we live it at all? I gave up at last, tossed the wrench a couple more times and quit. And quitting, was suddenly glad, all at once happy that I was where I was and knew what I knew even though it wasn't the answer to all existence or even a few illusions.

When I'm alone sometimes I sing. *"Oh, me and ol' PAINT!..."* I sang, patting the wing of the Fleet in true love for the thing (remember there was nobody to hear), *"We'll wander the sky...Hoppin' 'round hayfields till one of us gives in..."* Music and words both I compose as I go along. *"An' it won't be me givin' in, Paint... Unless you break a SPAR... and then I'll just tie you up with baling WIRE... and we'll go flying on... WE'LL GO FLYIN' ON..."*

The verses are endless when I get going and happy, since the rhyming isn't that critical. I had stopped thinking about the problems of the messiah; there was no way I could figure who he was or what he meant, and so I stopped trying and I guess that's what made me happy.

Long about ten o'clock the fire ran down and so did my song.

"Wherever you are, Donald Shimoda," I said, unrolling my blanket under the wing, "I wish you happy flying and no crowds. If that is what you want. No, I take that back. I wish, dear lonely messiah, that you find whatever it is that you want to find."

His handbook fell out of the pocket as I took off my shirt, and I read it where it opened.

The bond
that links your true family
is not one of blood, but
of respect and joy in
each other's life.

Rarely do members
of one family grow up
under the same
roof.

I didn't see how that applied to me, and reminded myself never to let a book replace my own thinking. I rustled down under the blanket, and then I was out like a bulb turned off, warm and dreamless under the sky and under several thousand stars that were illusions, maybe, but pretty ones, for sure.

When I came conscious again it was just sunrise, rose light and gold shadows. I woke not because of the light but because something was touching my head, ever so gently. I took it for a hay-stem, floating there. Second time I knew it was a bug, swatted wildly and nearly broke my hand...a nine-sixteenths end-wrench is a hard chunk of iron to swat full speed, and I woke up fast. The wrench bounced off the aileron hinge, buried itself for a moment in the grass, then floated grandly to hover in the air again. Then as I watched, coming wide awake, it sank softly back down to the ground and was still. By the time I thought to pick it up, it was the same old nine-sixteenths I knew and loved, just as heavy, just as eager to get at all those pesky nuts and bolts.

"Well, hell!"

I never say hell or damn – carryover from an ego thing as a child. But I was truly puzzled, and there was nothing else to say. What was happening to my wrench? Donald Shimoda was sixty miles at least over some horizon from here. I hefted the thing, examined it, balanced it, feeling like a prehistoric ape that cannot understand a wheel is turning before its very eyes. There had to be some simple reason...

I gave up at last, annoyed, put it on the toolbag and lit the fire for my pan-bread. There was no rush to go anywhere. Might stay here all day, if I felt like it.

The bread had risen well in the pan, was just ready to be turned when I heard a sound in the sky to the west.

There was no way that the sound could have been Shimoda's airplane, no way anybody could have tracked me to this one field out of millions of midwest fields, but I knew that it was him and started whistling... watching the bread and the sky and trying to think of something very calm to say when he landed.

It was the Travel Air, all right, flew in low over the Fleet, pulled up steep in a show-off turn, slipped down through the air and landed 60 mph, the speed a Travel Air ought to land. He pulled alongside and shut down his engine. I didn't say anything. Waved, but didn't say a word. I did stop whistling.

He got out of the cockpit and walked to the fire. "Hi, Richard."

"You're late," I said. "Almost burned the pan-bread."

"Sorry."

I handed him a cup of stream water and a tin plate with half the pan-bread and a chunk of margarine.

"How'd it go?" I said.

"Went OK," he said with an instant's half-smile. "I escaped with my life."

"Had some doubts you would."

He ate the bread for a while in silence. "You know," he said at last, contemplating his meal, "this is really terrible stuff."

"Nobody says you have to eat my pan-bread," I said crossly.

"Why does everybody hate my pan-bread? NOBODY LIKES MY PAN-BREAD! Why is that, Ascended Master?"

"Well," he grinned, "– and I'm speaking as God, now – I'd say that you believe that it's good and that therefore it does taste good to you. Try it without deeply believing what you believe and it's sort of like...a fire...after a flood...in a flourmill, don't you think? You meant to put the grass in, I guess."

"Sorry. Fell in off my sleeve, somehow. But don't you think the basic bread itself – not the grass or the little charred part, there – the basic pan-bread, don't you think...?"

"Terrible," he said, handing me back all but a bite of what I had handed to him. "I'd rather starve. Still have the peaches?"

"In the box."

How had he found me, in this field? A twenty-eight-foot wingspan in ten thousand miles of prairie farmland is not an easy target, looking into the sun, especially. But I vowed not to ask. If he wanted to tell me, he would tell me.

"How did you find me?" I said. "I could have landed anywhere."

He had opened the peach can and was eating peaches with a knife...not an easy trick.

"Like attracts like," he muttered, missing a peach slice.

"Oh?"

"Cosmic law."

"Oh."

I finished my bread and then scraped the pan with sand from the stream. That sure is good bread.

"Do you mind explaining? How is it that I am like your esteemed self? Or did by 'like' you mean the airplanes are alike, sort of?"

"We miracle-workers got to stick together," he said. The sentence was both kind and horrifying the way he said it.

"Ah...Don? Referring to your last comment? Perhaps you'd like to tell me what you had in mind: *we* miracle-workers?"

"From the position of the nine-sixteenths on the toolbag, I'd say you were running the old levitate-the-end-wrench trick this morning. Tell me if I'm wrong."

"Wasn't running anything! I woke up...the thing woke me up, by itself!"

"Oh. By itself." He was laughing at me.

"YES BY ITSELF!"

"Your understanding of your miracle-working, Richard, is as thorough as your understanding of bread-baking."

I didn't reply to that, just eased myself down on my bedroll and was quiet as could be. If he had something to say, he could say it in his own good time.

"Some of us start learning these things subconsciously. Our waking mind won't accept it, so we do our miracles in our sleep." He watched the sky, and the first little clouds of the day. "Don't be impatient, Richard. We're all on our way to learning more. It will come to you a little faster now, and you'll be a wise old spiritual maestro before you know it."

"What do you mean, before I know it? I don't *want* to know it! I don't want to know anything!"

"You don't want to know anything."

"Well, I want to know why the world is and what it is and why

69

I live here and where I'm going next: . . I want to know that. How to fly without an airplane, if I had a wish."

"Sorry."

"Sorry what?"

"Doesn't work that way. If you learn what this world is, how it works, you automatically start getting miracles, what will be called miracles. But of course nothing is miraculous. Learn what the magician knows and it's not magic anymore." He looked away from the sky. "You're like everybody else. You already know this stuff, you're just not aware that you know it, yet."

"I don't recall," I said, "I don't recall your asking me whether I want to learn this thing, whatever it is that has brought you crowds and misery all your life. Seems to have slipped my mind." Soon as I said the words I knew that he was going to say I'd remember later, and that he'd be right.

He stretched out in the grass, the last of the flour in its bag for a pillow. "Look, you don't worry about the crowds. They can't touch you unless you want them to. You're magic, remember: *FOOF!* – you're invisible, and walk through the doors."

"Crowd got you at Troy, didn't it?"

"Did I say I didn't want them to? I allowed that. I liked it. There's a little ham in all of us or we'd never make it as masters."

"But didn't you quit? Didn't I read . . . ?"

"The way things were going, I was turning into the One-and-Only Full-Time Messiah, and that job I quit cold. But I can't unlearn what I've spent lifetimes coming to know, can I?"

I closed my eyes and crunched a hay-stem. "Look, Donald, what are you trying to tell me? Why don't you come right out and say what is going on?"

70

It was quiet for a long time, and then he said, "Maybe you ought to tell me. You tell me what I'm trying to say, and I'll correct you if you're wrong."

I thought about that a minute, and decided to surprise him. "OK, I'll tell you." I practiced then pausing, to see how long he could wait if what I said didn't come out too fluent. The sun was high enough now to be warm, and way off in some hidden field a farmer worked a diesel tractor, cultivating corn on Sunday.

"OK, I'll tell you. First of all, it was no coincidence when I first saw you landed down in the field at Ferris, right?"

He was quiet as the hay growing.

"And second of all, you and I have some kind of mystical agreement which apparently I have forgotten and you haven't."

Only a soft wind blowing, and the distant tractor-sound wafting back and forth with it.

There was part of me listening that didn't think what I said was fiction. I was making up a true story.

"I'm going to say that we met three or four thousand years ago, give or take a day. We like the same kind of adventures, we probably hate the same sort of destroyers, learn with about as much fun, about as fast as each other. You've got a better memory. Our meeting again is what you mean by 'Like attracts like,' that you said."

I picked a new hay-stem. "How am I doing?"

"For a while I thought it was going to be a long haul," he said. "It is going to be a long haul, but I think there's a slim outside chance that you might make it this time. Keep talking."

"For another thing, I don't have to keep talking, because you already know what things people know. But if I didn't say these

71

things, you wouldn't know what I think that I know, and without that I can't learn any of the things I want to learn." I put down my hay-stem. "What's in it for you, Don? Why do you bother with people like me? Whenever somebody is advanced as you are, he gets all these miracle-powers as byproducts. You don't need me, you don't need anything at all from this world."

I turned my head and looked at him. His eyes were closed. "Like gas in the Travel Air?" he said.

"Right," I said. "So all there is left in the world is boredom...there are no adventures when you know that you can't be troubled by any thing on this earth. Your only problem is that you don't have any problems!"

That, I thought, was a terrific piece of talking.

"You missed, there," he said. "Tell me why I quit my job...do you know why I quit the Messiah job?"

"Crowds, you said. Everybody wanting you to do their miracles for them."

"Yeah. Not the first, the second. Crowdophobia is your cross, not mine. It's not crowds that wear me, it's the kind of crowd that doesn't care at all about what I came to say. You can walk New York to London on the ocean, you can pull gold coins out of forever and still not make them care, you know?"

When he said that, he looked lonelier than I had ever seen a man still alive. He didn't need food or shelter or money or fame. He was dying of his need to say what he knew, and nobody cared enough to listen.

I frowned at him, so as not to cry. "Well, you asked for it," I said. "If your happiness depends on what somebody else does, I guess you do have a problem."

72

He jerked his head up and his eyes blazed as though I had hit him with the wrench. I thought all at once that I would not be wise to get this guy mad at me. A man fries quick, struck by lightning.

Then he smiled that half-second smile. "You know what, Richard?" he said slowly. "You...are...*right!*"

He was quiet again, tranced, almost, by what I had said. Not noticing, I went on talking to him for hours about how we had met and what there was to learn, all these ideas firing through my head like morning comets and daylight meteors. He lay very still in the grass, not moving, not saying a word. By noon I finished my version of the universe and all things that dwelled therein.

"...and I feel like I've barely begun, Don, there's so much to say. How do I know all this? How come is that?"

He didn't answer.

"If you expect me to answer my own question, I confess that I do not know. Why can I say all these things now, when I've never even tried, before? What has happened to me?"

No answer.

"Don? It's OK for you to talk now, please."

He didn't say a word. I had explained the panorama of life to him, and my messiah, as though he had heard all he needed in that one chance word about his happiness, had fallen fast asleep.

7

WEDNESDAY morning, it's six o'clock, I'm not awake and *WHOOM!!* there's this enormous noise sudden and violent as some high-explosive symphony; instant thousand-voice choirs, words in Latin, violins and tympani and trumpets to shatter glass. The ground shuddered, the Fleet rocked on her wheels and I came out from under the wing like a 400-volt cat, fur straight-out exclamation points.

The sky was cold-fire sunrise, the clouds alive in wild paint, but all of it blurred in the dynamite crescendo.

"STOP IT! STOP IT! OFF THE MUSIC, *OFF* IT!!"

Shimoda yelled so loud and so furious I could hear him over the din, and the sound stopped at once, echoes rolling off and away and away and away. Then it was a gentle holy song, quiet as the breeze, Beethoven in a dream.

He was unimpressed. "LOOK, I SAID OFF IT!!"

The music stopped.

"Whuf!" he said.

I just looked at him.

"There is a time and a place for everything, right?" he said.

"Well, time and place, well..."

"A little celestial music is fine, in the privacy of your own mind, and maybe on special occasions, but the first thing in the morning, and turned up that loud? What are you doing?"

"What am *I* doing? Don, I was sound asleep...what do you mean, what am *I* doing?"

He shook his head, shrugged his shoulders helplessly, snorted and went back to his sleeping bag under the wing.

The handbook was upside down in the grass where it had fallen. I turned it over carefully, and read.

Argue
for your limitations,
and sure enough,
they're
yours.

There was a lot I didn't understand about messiahs.

8

WE FINISHED the day in Hammond, Wisconsin, flying a few Monday passengers, then we walked to town for dinner, and started back.

"Don, I will grant you that this life can be interesting or dull or whatever we choose to make it. But even in my brilliant times I have never been able to figure out why we're here in the first place. Tell me something about that."

We passed the hardware store (closed) and the movie theater (open: *Butch Cassidy and the Sundance Kid*), and instead of answering he stopped, turned back on the sidewalk.

"You have money, don't you?"

"Lots. What's the matter?"

"Let's see the show," he said. "You buy?"

"I don't know, Don. You go ahead. I'll get back to the airplanes. Don't like to leave 'em alone too long." What was suddenly so important about a motion picture?

"The planes are OK. Let's go to the show."

"It's already started."

"So we come in late."

He was already buying his ticket. I followed him into the dark and we sat down near the back of the theater. There might have been fifty people around us in the gloom.

I forgot about why we came, after a while, and got caught up in the story, which I've always thought is a classic movie, anyway; this would be my third time seeing *Sundance*. The time in the theater spiraled and stretched the way it does in a good film, and I watched awhile for technical reasons...how each scene was designed and fit to the next, why this scene now and not later on. I tried to look at it that way, but got spun up in the story and forgot.

About the part where Butch and Sundance are surrounded by the entire Bolivian army, almost at the end, Shimoda touched my shoulder. I leaned toward him, watching the movie, wishing he could have kept whatever he was going to say till after it was over.

"Richard?"

"Yeah."

"Why are you here?"

"It's a good movie, Don. *Sh.*" Butch and Sundance, blood all over them, were talking about why they ought to go to Australia.

"Why is it good?" he said.

"It's fun. *Sh.* I'll tell you later."

"Snap out of it. Wake up. It's all illusions."

I was irked. "Donald, there's just a few minutes more and then we can talk all you want. But let me watch the movie, OK?"

He whispered intensely, dramatically. "Richard, *why are you here?*"

"Look, I'm here because you asked me to come in here!" I turned back and tried to watch the end.

"You didn't have to come, you could have said no thank you."

"I LIKE THE MOVIE..." A man in front turned to look at me for a second. "I like the movie, Don; is there anything wrong with that?"

"Nothing at all," he said, and he didn't say another word till it was over and we were walking again past the used-tractor lot and out into the dark toward the field and the airplanes. It would be raining, before long.

I thought about his odd behavior in the theater. "You do everything for a reason, Don?"

"Sometimes."

"Why the movie? Why did you all of a sudden want to see *Sundance*?"

"You asked a question."

"Yes. Do you have an answer?"

"That is my answer. We went to the movie because you asked a question. The movie was the answer to your question."

He was laughing at me, I knew it.

"What was my question?"

There was a long pained silence. "Your question, Richard, was

78

that even in your brilliant times you have never been able to figure out why we are here."

I remembered. "And the movie was my answer."

"Yes."

"Oh."

"You don't understand," he said.

"No."

"That was a good movie," he said, "but the world's best movie is still an illusion, is it not? The pictures aren't even moving; they only appear to move. Changing light that seems to move across a flat screen set up in the dark?"

"Well, yes." I was beginning to understand.

"The other people, any people anywhere who go to any movie show, why are they there, when it is only illusions?"

"Well, it's entertainment," I said.

"Fun. That's right. One."

"Could be educational."

"Good. It is always that. Learning. Two."

"Fantasy, escape."

"That's fun, too. One."

"Technical reasons. To see how a film is made."

"Learning. Two."

"Escape from boredom..."

"Escape. You said that."

"Social. To be with friends," I said.

"Reason for going, but not for seeing the film. That's fun, anyway. One."

79

Whatever I came up with fit his two fingers; people see films for fun or for learning or for both together.

"And a movie is like a lifetime, Don, is that right?"

"Yes."

"Then why would anybody choose a bad lifetime, a horror movie?"

"They not only come to the horror movie for fun, they know it is going to be a horror movie when they walk in," he said.

"But why?..."

"Do you like horror films?"

"No."

"Do you ever see them?"

"No."

"But some people spend a lot of money and time to see horror, or soap-opera problems that to other people are dull and boring?..." He left the question for me to answer.

"Yes."

"You don't have to see their films and they don't have to see yours. That is called 'freedom.'"

"But why would anybody want to be horrified? Or bored?"

"Because they think they deserve it for horrifying somebody else, or they like the excitement of horrification, or that boring is the way they think films have to be. Can you believe that lots of people for reasons that are very sound to them enjoy believing that they are helpless in their own films? No, you can't."

"No, I can't," I said.

"Until you understand that, you will wonder why some

people are unhappy. They are unhappy because they have chosen to be unhappy, and, Richard, that is all right!"

"Hm."

"We are game-playing, fun-having creatures, we are the otters of the universe. We cannot die, we cannot hurt ourselves any more than illusions on the screen can be hurt. But we can believe we're hurt, in whatever agonizing detail we want. We can believe we're victims, killed and killing, shuddered around by good luck and bad luck."

"Many lifetimes?" I asked.

"How many movies have you seen?"

"Oh."

"Films about living on this planet, about living on other planets; anything that's got space and time is all movie and all illusion," he said. "But for a while we can learn a huge amount and have a lot of fun with our illusions, can we not?"

"How far do you take this movie thing, Don?"

"How far do you want? You saw the film tonight partly because I wanted to see it. Lots of people choose lifetimes because they enjoy doing things together. The actors in the film tonight have played together in other films – before or after depends on which film you've seen first, or you can see them at the same time on different screens. We buy tickets to these films, paying admission by agreeing to believe in the reality of space and the reality of time . . . Neither one is true, but anyone who doesn't want to pay that price cannot appear on this planet, or in any space-time system at all."

81

"Are there some people who don't have any lifetimes at all in space-time?"

"Are there some people who never go to movies?"

"I see. They get their learning in different ways?"

"Right you are," he said, pleased with me. "Space-time is a fairly primitive school. But a lot of people stay with the illusion even if it is boring, and they don't want the lights turned on early."

"Who writes these movies, Don?"

"Isn't it strange how much we know if only we ask ourselves instead of somebody else? Who writes these movies, Richard?"

"We do," I said.

"Who acts?"

"Us."

"Who's the cameraman, the projectionist, the theater manager, the ticket-taker, the distributor, and who watches them all happen? Who is free to walk out in the middle, any time, change the plot whenever, who is free to see the same film over and over again?"

"Let me guess," I said. "Anybody who wants to?"

"Is that enough freedom for you?" he said.

"And is that why movies are so popular? That we instinctively know they are a parallel of our own lifetimes?"

"Maybe so...maybe not. Doesn't matter much, does it? What's the projector?"

"Mind," I said. "No. Imagination. It's our imagination, no matter what you say."

"What's the film?" he asked.

"Got me."

"Whatever we give our consent to put into our imagination?"

"Maybe so, Don."

"You can hold a reel of film in your hands," he said, "and it's all finished and complete – beginning, middle, end are all there that same second, the same millionths of a second. The film exists beyond the time that it records, and if you know what the movie is, you know generally what's going to happen before you walk into the theater: there's going to be battles and excitement, winners and losers, romance, disaster; you know that's all going to be there. But in order to get caught up and swept away in it, in order to enjoy it to its most, you have to put it in a projector and let it go through the lens minute by minute . . . any illusion requires space and time to be experienced. So you pay your nickel and you get your ticket and you settle down and forget what's going on outside the theater and the movie begins for you."

"And nobody's really hurt? That's just tomato-sauce blood?"

"No, it's blood all right," he said. "But it might as well be tomato sauce for the effect it has on our real life . . ."

"And reality?"

"Reality is divinely indifferent, Richard. A mother doesn't care what part her child plays in his games; one day bad-guy, next day good-guy. The Is doesn't even know about our illusions and games. It only knows Itself, and us in its likeness, perfect and finished."

"I'm not sure I want to be perfect and finished. Talk about boredom . . ."

83

"Look at the sky," he said, and it was such a quick subject-change that I looked at the sky. There was some broken cirrus, way up high, the first bit of moonlight silvering the edges.

"Pretty sky," I said.

"It is a perfect sky?"

"Well, it's always a perfect sky, Don."

"Are you telling me that even though it's changing every second, the sky is always a perfect sky?"

"Gee, I'm smart. Yes!"

"And the sea is always a perfect sea, and it's always changing, too," he said. "If perfection is stagnation, then heaven is a swamp! And the Is ain't hardly no swamp-cookie."

"*Isn't* hardly no swamp-cookie," I corrected, absently. "Perfect, and all the time changing. Yeah. I'll buy that."

"You bought it a long time ago, if you insist on time."

I turned to him as we walked. "Doesn't it get boring for you, Don, staying on just this one dimension?"

"Oh. Am I staying on just this one dimension?" he said. "Are you?"

"Why is it that everything I say is wrong?"

"Is everything you say wrong?" he said.

"I think I'm in the wrong business."

"You think maybe real estate?" he said.

"Real estate or insurance."

"There's a future in real estate, if you want one."

"OK. I'm sorry," I said. "I don't want a future. Or a past. I'd

just as soon become a nice old Master of the World of Illusion.
Looks like maybe in another week?"

"Well, Richard, I hope not *that* long!"

I looked at him carefully, but he wasn't smiling.

9

THE DAYS blurred one into another. We flew as always, but I had stopped counting summer by the names of towns or the money we earned from passengers. I began counting the summer by the things I learned, the talks we had when flying was done, and by the miracles that happened now and then along the way to the time I knew at last that they aren't miracles at all.

Imagine
the universe beautiful
and just and
perfect,

the handbook said to me once.

*T*hen be sure of one thing:
the *I*s has imagined it
quite a bit better
than you
have.

10

THE AFTERNOON was quiet... an occasional passenger now and then. Time between I practiced vaporizing clouds.

I have been a flight instructor, and I know that students always make easy things hard; I do know better, yet there was I a student again, frowning fiercely at my cumulus targets. I needed more teaching, for once, than practice. Shimoda was stretched out under the Fleet's wing, pretending to be asleep. I kicked him softly on the arm, and he opened his eyes.

"I can't do it," I said.

"Yes you can," he said, and closed his eyes again.

"Don, I've tried! Just when I think something's happening, the cloud strikes back and goes poufing up bigger than ever."

He sighed and sat up. "Pick me a cloud. An easy one, please."

I chose the biggest meanest cloud in the sky, three thousand feet tall, bursting up white smoke from hell. "The one over the silo, yonder," I said. "The one that's going black now."

He looked at me in silence. "Why is it you hate me?"

"It's because I like you, Don, that I ask these things." I smiled. "You need challenge. If you'd rather, I could pick something smaller..."

He sighed again and turned back to the sky. "I'll try. Now, which one?"

I looked, and the cloud, the monster with its million tons of rain, was gone; just an ungainly blue-sky hole where it had been.

"Yike," I said quietly.

"A job worth doing..." he quoted. "No, much as I would like to accept the praise which you heap upon me, I must in all honesty tell you this: it's easy."

He pointed to a little puff of a cloud overhead. "There. Your turn. Ready? Go."

I looked at the wisp of a thing, and it looked back at me. I thought it gone, thought an empty place where it was, poured visions of heat-rays up at it, asked it to reappear somewhere else, and slowly slowly, in one minute, in five, in seven, the cloud at last was gone. Other clouds got bigger, mine went away.

"You're not very fast, are you?" he said.

"That was my first time! I'm just beginning! Up against the

impossible...well, the improbable, and all you can think to say is I'm not very fast. That was brilliant and you know it!"

"Amazing. You were so attached to it, and still it disappeared for you."

"Attached! I was whocking that cloud with everything I had! Fireballs, laser beams, vacuum cleaner a block high..."

"Negative attachments, Richard. If you really want to remove a cloud from your life, you do not make a big production out of it, you just relax and remove it from your thinking. That's all there is to it."

A cloud does not know why it moves in just such a direction and at such a speed,

was what the handbook had to say.

It feels an impulsion... this is
the place to go now. **B**ut the sky knows
the reasons and the patterns
behind all clouds,
and you will know, too, when
you lift yourself high enough
to see beyond
horizons.

91

11

*You are
never given a wish
without also being given the
power to make it true.
You may
have to work for it,
however.*

We had landed in a huge grazing place next to a three-acre horse-pond, away from towns, somewhere along the line between Illinois and Indiana. No passengers; it was our day off, I thought.

"Listen," he said. "Don't listen. Just stay there quiet and watch. What you are going to see is not any miracle. Read your atomic-physics book...a child can walk on water."

He told me this, and as though he didn't notice the water was even there, he turned and walked out some yards from shore, on the surface of the horse-pond. What it looked like, was that the pond was a hot-summer mirage over a lake of stone. He stood firm on the surface, not a wave or ripple splashed over his flying-boots.

"Here," he said. "Come do it."

I saw it with my eyes. It was possible, obviously, because there he stood, so I walked out to join him. It felt like walking on clear blue linoleum, and I laughed.

"Donald, what are you doing to me?"

"I am merely showing you what everybody learns, sooner or later," he said, "and you're handy now."

"But I'm..."

"Look. The water can be solid" – he stamped his foot and the sound was leather on rock – "or not." He stamped again and water splashed over us both. "Got the feel of that? Try it."

How quickly we get used to miracles! In less than a minute I began to think that walking on water is possible, is natural, is...well, so what?

"But if the water is solid now, how can we drink it?"

"Same way we walk on it, Richard. *It* isn't solid, and *it* isn't liquid. You and I decide what it's going to be for us. If you want water to be liquid, think it liquid, act as if it's liquid, drink it. If you want it to be air, act as if it's air, breathe it. Try."

Maybe it's something about the presence of an advanced soul, I thought. Maybe these things are allowed to happen in a certain radius, fifty feet in a circle around them...

I knelt on the surface and dipped my hand into the pond. Liquid. Then I lay down and put my face into the blue of it and breathed, trusting. It breathed like warm liquid oxygen, no choking or gasping. I sat up and looked a question at him, expecting him to know what was in my mind.

"Speak," he said.

"Why do I have to speak?"

"For what you have to say, it's more precise to talk in words. Speak."

"If we can walk on water, and breathe it and drink it, why can't we do the same to land?"

"Yes. Good. You will notice..."

He walked to the shore easily as walking a painted lake. But when his feet touched the ground, the sand and grass at the edge, he began to sink, until with a few slow steps he was up to his shoulders in earth and grass. It was as though the pond had suddenly become an island, and the land about had turned to sea. He swam for a moment in the pasture, splashing it about him in dark loam drops, then floated on top of it, then rose and walked on it. It was suddenly miraculous to see a man *walking on the ground!*

I stood on the pond and applauded his performance. He bowed, and applauded mine.

I walked to the edge of the pond, thought the earth to liquid and touched it with my toe. Ripples spread into the grass in rings. How deep is the ground? I nearly asked aloud. The ground will be as deep as I think it will be. Two feet deep, I thought, it will be two feet deep, and I'll wade.

I stepped confidently into the shore and sank over my head, an instant dropoff. It was black underground, scary, and I fought to the surface, holding my breath, flailing out for some solid water, for the edge of the pond to hold on to.

He sat on the grass and laughed.

"You are a remarkable student, do you know that?"

"I ain't no student at all! Get me out of here!"

"Get yourself out."

95

I stopped struggling. I see it solid and I can climb right out. I see it solid...and I climbed out, caked and crusted in black dirt.

"Man, you really get dirty doing this!"

His own blue shirt and jeans were without spot or mote of dust.

"*Aaaa!*" I shook the dirt out of my hair, flapped it out of my ears. Finally I put my wallet on the grass, walked into the liquid water and cleaned myself the traditional wet way.

"I know there's a better way to get clean than this."

"There's a faster way, yes."

"Don't tell me, of course. Just sit there and laugh and let me figure it all out for myself."

"OK."

I finally had to walk squishing back to the Fleet and change clothes, hanging the wet stuff on the flying wires to dry.

"Richard, don't forget what you did today. It is easy to forget our times of knowing, to think they've been dreams or old miracles, one time. Nothing good is a miracle, nothing lovely is a dream."

"The world is a dream, you say, and it's lovely, sometimes. Sunset. Clouds. Sky."

"No. The image is a dream. The beauty is real. Can you see the difference?"

I nodded, almost understanding. Later I sneaked a look in the handbook.

*The world
is your exercise-book, the pages
on which you do your sums.
It is not reality,
although you can express reality
there if you wish. You are also
free to write nonsense,
or lies, or to tear
the pages.*

12

The
original sin is to
limit the Is.
*D*on't.

I T WAS an easy warm afternoon between rain-showers, sidewalks wet on our way out of town.

"You can walk through walls, can't you, Don?"

"No."

"When you say no to something I know is yes, that means you don't like the way I said the question."

"We certainly are observant, aren't we?" he said.

"Is the problem with *walk* or with *walls*?"

"Yes, and worse. Your question presumes that I exist in one limited place-time and move to another place-time. Today I'm not in the mood to accept your presumptions about me."

I frowned. He knew what I was asking. Why didn't he just answer me straight and let me get on to finding out how he does these things?

"That's my little way of helping you be precise in your thinking," he said mildly.

"OK. You can make it appear that you can walk through walls, if you want. Is that a better question?"

"Yes. Better. But if you want to be precise..."

"Don't tell me. I know how to say what I mean. Here is my question. How is it that you can move the illusion of a limited sense of identity, expressed in this belief of a space-time continuum as your 'body,' through the illusion of material restriction that is called a 'wall'?"

"Well done!" he said. "When you ask the question properly it answers itself, doesn't it?"

"No, the question hasn't answered itself. How do you walk through walls?"

"RICHARD! You had it nearly right and then blew it all to pieces! I cannot walk through walls...when you say that, you're assuming things I don't assume at all, and if I do assume them, the answer is, 'I can't.'"

"But it's so hard to put everything so precisely, Don. Don't you know what I mean?"

"So just because something is hard, you don't try to do it? Walking was hard at first, but you practiced at it and now you make it look easy."

I sighed. "Yeah. OK. Forget the question."

"I'll forget it. My question is, can you?" He looked at me as though he hadn't a care in the world.

"So you're saying that body is illusion and wall is illusion but identity is real and that can't be hemmed by illusions."

99

"I'm not saying that. You're saying that."

"But it's true."

"Naturally," he said.

"How do you do it?"

"Richard, you don't do anything. You see it done already, and it is."

"Gee, that sounds easy."

"It's like walking. You wonder how it ever came hard for you to learn."

"Don, walking through walls, it isn't hard for me now; it is impossible."

"Do you think that maybe if you say *impossible* over and over again a thousand times that suddenly hard things will come easy for you?"

"I'm sorry. It is possible, and I'll do it when it is right for me to do it."

"He walks on water, folks, and he is discouraged because he doesn't walk through walls."

"But that was easy, and this..."

"Argue for your limitations and you get to keep them," he sang. "Did you not a week ago swim in the earth itself?"

"I did that."

"And is not *wall* just vertical earth? Does it matter that much to you which direction the illusion runs? Horizontal illusions are conquerable, but vertical illusions aren't?"

"I think you're getting through to me, Don."

He looked at me and smiled. "The time I get through to you is the time to leave you alone for a while."

The last building in town was a feed and grain warehouse, a big place built of orange brick. It was almost as if he had decided to take a different way back to the airplanes, turning down some secret shortcut alley. The shortcut was through the brick wall. He turned abruptly to the right, into the wall, and he was gone. I think now that if I had turned at once with him, I could have gone through it, too. But I just stopped on the sidewalk and looked at the place where he had been. When I put out my hand and touched the brick, it was solid brick.

"Some day, Donald," I said. "Some day..." I walked alone the long way back to the airplanes.

"Donald," I said when I got to the field, "I have come to the conclusion that you just don't live in this world."

He looked at me startled from the top of his wing, where he was learning to pour gas into the tank. "Of course not. Can you tell me one person who does?"

"What do you mean, can I tell you one person who does. ME! *I* live in this world!"

"Excellent," he said, as though through independent study I had uncovered a hidden mystery. "Remind me to buy you lunch today... I marvel at the way you never stop learning."

I puzzled over that. He wasn't being sarcastic or ironic; he had meant just what he said. "What do you mean? Of course I live in this world. Me and about four billion other people. It's *you* who..."

101

"Oh, God, Richard! You're serious! Cancel the lunch. No hamburger, no malt, no nothing at all! Here I had thought you had reached this major knowing – " He broke off and looked down on me in angry pity. "You're sure of that. You live in the same world, do you, as . . . a stockbroker, shall we say? Your life has just been all tumbled and changed, I presume, by the new SEC policy – mandatory review of portfolios with shareholder investment loss more than fifty percent? You live in the same world as a tournament chess player, do you? With the New York Open going on this week, Petrosian and Fischer and Browne in Manhattan for a half-million-dollar purse, what are you doing in a hayfield in Maitland, Ohio? You with your 1929 Fleet biplane landed on a farm field, with your major life priorities farmers' permission, people who want ten-minute airplane rides, Kinner aircraft engine maintenance and mortal fear of hailstorms . . . how many people do you think live in your world? You say four *billion* people live in your world? Are you standing way down there on the ground and telling me that four billion people do not live in four billion separate worlds, are you going to put that across on me?" He panted from his fast talking.

"I could almost taste that hamburger, with the cheese melting . . . " I said.

"I'm sorry. I would have been so happy to buy. But, ah, that's over and done now, best forgotten."

Though it was the last time I accused him of not living in this world, it took me a long time to understand the words where the handbook opened:

*If
you will
practice being fictional
for a while, you will understand
that fictional characters are
sometimes more real than
people with bodies
and heartbeats.*

13

*Your
conscience is
the measure of the
honesty of your selfishness.
Listen to it
carefully.*

W E ARE ALL FREE to do whatever we want to do," he said that night. "Isn't that simple and clean and clear? Isn't that a great way to run a universe?"

"Almost. You forgot a pretty important part," I said.

"Oh?"

"We are all free to do what we want to do, as long as we don't hurt somebody else," I chided. "I know you meant that, but you ought to say what you mean."

There was a sudden shambling sound in the dark, and I looked at him quickly. "Did you hear that?"

"Yeah. Sounds like there's somebody..." He got up, walked into the dark. He laughed suddenly, said a name I couldn't catch. "It's OK," I heard him say. "No, we'd be glad to have you...no need you standing around...come on, you're welcome, really..."

The voice was heavily accented, not quite Russian, nor Czech, more Transylvanian. "Thank you. I do not wish to impose myself upon your evening..."

The man he brought with him to the firelight was, well, he was unusual to find in a midwest night. A small lean wolflike fellow, frightening to the eye, dressed in evening clothes, a black cape lined in red satin, he was uncomfortable in the light.

"I was passing by," he said. "The field is a shortcut to my house..."

"Is it?" Shimoda did not believe the man, knew he was lying, and at the same time did all he could to keep from laughing out loud. I hoped to understand before long.

"Make yourself comfortable," I said. "Can we help you at all?" I really didn't feel that helpful, but he was so shrinking, I did want him to be at ease, if he could.

He looked on me with a desperate smile that turned me to ice. "Yes, you can help me. I need this very much or I would not ask. May I drink your blood? Just some? It is my food, I need human blood..."

Maybe it was the accent, he didn't know English that well or I didn't understand his words, but I was on my feet quicker than I had been in many a month, hay flying into the fire from my quickness.

The man stepped back. I am generally harmless, but I am not a small person and I could have looked threatening. He turned his head away. "Sir, I am sorry! I am sorry! Please forget that I said anything about blood! But you see..."

"What are you saying?" I was the more fierce because I was scared. "What in the *hell* are you saying, mister? I don't know what you are, are you some kind of VAM–?"

Shimoda cut me off before I could say the word. "Richard, our guest was talking, and you interrupted. Please go ahead, sir; my friend is a little hasty."

"Donald," I said, "this guy..."

"*Be quiet!*"

That surprised me so much that I was quiet, and looked a sort of terrified question at the man, caught from his native darkness into our firelight.

"Please to understand. I did not choose to be born vampire. Is unfortunate. I do not have many friends. But I must have a certain small amount of fresh blood every night or I writhe in terrible pain, longer than that without it and I cannot live! Please, I will be deeply hurt – I will die – if you do not allow me to suck your blood...just a small amount, more than a pint I do not need." He advanced a step toward me, licking his lips, thinking that Shimoda somehow controlled me and would make me submit.

"One more step and there will be blood, all right. Mister, you touch me and you die..." I wouldn't have killed him, but I did want to tie him up, at least, before we talked much more.

He must have believed me, for he stopped and sighed. He turned to Shimoda. "You have made your point?"

"I think so. Thank you."

107

The vampire looked up at me and smiled, completely at ease, enjoying himself hugely, an actor on stage when the show is over. "I won't drink your blood, Richard," he said in perfect friendly English, no accent at all. As I watched he faded as though he was turning out his own light... in five seconds he had disappeared.

Shimoda sat down again by the fire. "Am I ever glad you don't mean what you say!"

I was still trembling with adrenalin, ready for my fight with a monster. "Don, I'm not sure I'm built for this. Maybe you'd better tell me what's going on. Like, for instance, what... was that?"

"Dot was a wompire from Tronsylwania," he said in words thicker than the creature's own. "Or to be more precise, dot was a *thought-form* of a wompire from Tronsylwania. If you ever want to make a point, you think somebody isn't listening, whip 'em up a little thought-form to demonstrate what you mean. Do you think I overdid him, with the cape and the fangs and the accent like that? Was he too scary for you?"

"The cape was first class, Don. But that was the most stereotyped, outlandish... I wasn't scared at all."

He sighed. "Oh well. But you got the point, at least, and that's what matters."

"What point?"

"Richard, in being so fierce toward my vampire, you were doing what you wanted to do, even though you thought it was going to hurt somebody else. He even *told* you he'd be hurt if..."

"He was going to suck my blood!"

"Which is what we do to anyone when we tell them we'll be hurt if they don't live our way."

I was quiet for a long time, thinking about that. I had always believed that we are free to do as we please only if we don't hurt another, and this didn't fit. There was something missing.

"The thing that puzzles you," he said, "is an accepted saying that happens to be impossible. The phrase is *hurt somebody else*. We choose, ourselves, to be hurt or not to be hurt, no matter what. Us who decides. Nobody else. My vampire told you he'd be hurt if you didn't let him? That's his decision to be hurt, that's his choice. What you do about it is your decision, your choice: give him blood; ignore him; tie him up; drive a stake of holly through his heart. If he doesn't want the holly stake, he's free to resist, in whatever way he wants. It goes on and on, choices, choices."

"When you look at it that way..."

"Listen," he said, "it's important. *We are all. Free. To do. Whatever. We want. To do.*"

14

*Every person,
all the events of your life
are there because you have
drawn them there.*

*What you choose
to do with them is
up to you.*

DON'T YOU get lonely, Don?" It was at the cafe in Ryerson, Ohio, that it occurred to me to ask him.

"I'm surprised you'd..."

"Sh," I said. "I haven't finished my question. Don't you ever get just a little lonely?"

"What you think as..."

"Wait. All these people, we see them just a few minutes. Once in a while there's a face in the crowd, some lovely star-bright woman who makes me want to stay and say hello, just be still and not moving and talk for a while. But she flies with me ten minutes or she doesn't and she's gone and next day I'm off to Shelbyville and I never see her again. That's lonely. But I guess I can't find lasting friends when I'm an unlasting one myself."

He was quiet.

"Or can I?"

"May I talk now?"

"I think so, yes." The hamburgers in this place were wrapped half-over in thin oiled paper, and when you unwrapped them you got sesame seeds everywhere – useless little things, but the

111

hamburgers were good. He ate in silence for a time and so did I, wondering what he would say.

"Well, Richard, we're magnets, aren't we? Not magnets. We're iron, wrapped in copper wire, and whenever we want to magnetize ourselves we can. Pour our inner voltage through the wire, we can attract whatever we want to attract. A magnet is not anxious about how it works. It is itself, and by its nature it draws some things and leaves others untouched."

I ate a potato chip and frowned at him. "You left out one thing. How do I do it?"

"You don't do anything. Cosmic law, remember? Like attracts like. Just be who you are, calm and clear and bright. Automatically, as we shine who we are, asking ourselves every minute is this what I really want to do, doing it only when we answer yes, automatically that turns away those who have nothing to learn from who we are and attracts those who do, and from whom we have to learn, as well."

"But that takes a lot of faith, and meanwhile you get pretty lonely."

He looked at me strangely over his hamburger. "Humbug on faith. Takes zero faith. What it takes is imagination." He swept the table between us clean, pushing salt and french fries out of the way, ketchup, forks and knives, so that I wondered what was going to happen, what would be materialized before my very eyes.

"If you have imagination as a grain of sesame seed," he said, herding an example seed to the middle of the clearing, "all things are possible to you."

I looked at the sesame seed, and then at him. "Wish you Messiahs would get together and agree. I thought the thing was faith, when the world goes against me."

112

"No. I wanted to correct that, when I was working, but it was a long uphill fight. Two thousand years ago, five thousand, they didn't have a word for imagination, and faith was the best they could come up with for a pretty solemn bunch of followers. Also, they didn't have sesame seeds."

I knew for a fact that they had sesame seeds, but I let this lie go past. "I'm supposed to imagine this magnetizing? I imagine some lovely wise mystical lady appearing in a hayfield crowd in Tarragon, Illinois? I can do that, but that's all that is, that's just my imagination."

He looked despairingly to heaven, represented for the moment by the tin-plate ceiling and cold lights of Em and Edna's Cafe. "Just your imagination? *Of course* it's your imagination! This world is your imagination, have you forgotten? *Where your thinking is, there is your experience; As a man thinks, so is he; That which I feared is come upon me; Think and grow rich: Creative visualization for fun and profit; How to find friends by being who you are.* Your imagining doesn't change the Is one whit, doesn't affect reality at all. But we are talking about Warner Brothers worlds, MGM lifetimes, and every second of those are illusions and imaginations. All dreams with the symbols we waking dreamers conjure for ourselves."

He lined his fork and knife as though he was building a bridge from his place to mine. "You wonder what your dreams say? Just as well you look at the things of your waking life and ask what they stand for. You with airplanes in your life, every time you turn around."

"Well, Don, yes." I wished he would slow down, not pile this on me all at once; mile a minute is too fast for new ideas.

"If you dreamed about airplanes, what would that mean to you?"

113

"Well, freedom. Airplane dreams are escape and flight and setting myself free."

"How clear do you want it? The dream awake is the same: your will to be free of all things that tie you back – routine, authority, boredom, gravity. What you haven't realized is that you're already free, and you always have been. If you had half the sesame seeds of this...you're already supreme lord of your magician's life. *Only* imagination! What are you saying?"

The waitress looked at him strangely from time to time, drying dishes, listening, puzzling over who this was.

"So you never get lonely, Don?" I said.

"Unless I feel like it. I have friends on other dimensions that are around me from time to time. So do you."

"No. I mean on this dimension, this imaginary world. Show me what you mean, give me a little miracle of the magnet...I do want to learn this."

"You show me," he said. "To bring anything into your life, imagine that it's already there."

"Like what? Like my lovely lady?"

"Anything. Not your lady. Something small, at first."

"I'm supposed to practice now?"

"Yes."

"OK....*A blue feather*."

He looked at me blankly. "Richard? A blue feather?"

"You said anything not a lady something little."

He shrugged. "Fine. A blue feather. Imagine the feather. Visualize it, every line and edge of it, the tip, V-splits where it's torn, fluff around the quill. Just for a minute. Then let it go."

I closed my eyes for a minute and saw an image in my mind,

five inches long, iridescing blue to silver at the edges. A bright clear feather floating there in the dark.

"Surround it in golden light, if you want. That's a healing thing, to help make it real, but it works in magnetizing, too."

I surrounded my feather in gold glow. "OK."

"That's it. You can open your eyes now."

I opened my eyes. "Where's my feather?"

"If you had it clear in your thought, it is even this moment barreling down on you like a Mack truck."

"My feather? Like a Mack truck?"

"Figuratively, Richard."

All that afternoon I looked for the feather to appear, and it didn't. It was evening, dinnertime over a hot turkey sandwich, that I saw it. A picture and small print on the carton of milk. *Packaged for Scott Dairies by Blue Feather Farms, Bryan, Ohio.* "Don! My feather!"

He looked, and shrugged his shoulders. "I thought you wanted the actual feather."

"Well, any feather for openers, don't you think?"

"Did you see just the feather all alone, or were you holding the feather in your hand?"

"All alone."

"That explains it. If you want to be with what you're magnetizing, you have to put yourself in the picture, too. Sorry I didn't say that."

A spooky strange feeling. It worked! I had consciously magnetized my first thing! "Today a feather," I said, "tomorrow the world!"

"Be careful, Richard," he said hauntingly, "or you'll be sorry..."

115

15

The
truth you
speak has no past
and no future. *It is,*
and that's all it
needs to be.

I LAY ON my back under the Fleet, wiping oil from the lower fuselage. Somehow the engine was throwing less oil now than it had thrown before. Shimoda flew one passenger, then came over and sat on the grass as I worked.

"Richard, how can you hope to impress the world when everybody else works for their living and you run around all irresponsible from day to day in your crazy biplane, selling passenger rides?" He was testing me again. "There's a question you are gonna get more than once."

"Well, Donald, Part One: I do not exist to impress the world. I exist to live my life in a way that will make me happy."

"OK. Part Two?"

117

"Part Two: Everybody else is free to do whatever they feel like doing, for a living. Part Three: Responsible is Able to Respond, able to answer for the way we choose to live. There's only one person we have to answer to, of course, and that is...?"

"...ourselves," Don said, replying for the imaginary crowd of seekers sitting around.

"We don't even have to answer to ourselves, if we don't feel like it...there's nothing wrong with being irresponsible. But most of us find it more interesting to know why we act as we do, why we make our choices just so – whether we choose to watch a bird or step on an ant or work for money at something we'd rather not be doing." I winced a little. "Is that too long an answer?"

He nodded. "Way too long."

"OK....How do you hope to impress the world..." I rolled out from under the plane and rested for a while in the shade of the wings. "How about I allow the world to live as it chooses, and I allow me to live as I choose."

He threw a happy proud smile at me. "Spoken like a true messiah! Simple, direct, quotable, and it doesn't answer the question unless somebody takes the time to think carefully about it."

"Try me some more." It was delicious, to watch my own mind work, when we did this.

"'Master,'" he said, "'I want to be loved, I'm kind, I do unto others as I would have them do unto me, but still I don't have any friends and I'm all alone.' How are you going to answer that one?"

"Beats me," I said. "I don't have the foggiest idea what to tell you."

"WHAT?"

"Just a little humor, Don, liven up the evening. A little harmless change-of-pacer, there."

"You'd best be plenty careful how you liven up the evenings. Problems are not jokes and games to the people who come to you, unless they are highly advanced themselves, and that sort know they're their own messiah. You are being given the answers, so speak them out. Try that 'Beats me' stuff and you'll see how fast a mob can burn a man at the stake."

I drew myself up proudly. "Seeker, thou comest to me for an answer, and unto thee I do answer: The Golden Rule doesn't work. How would you like to meet a masochist who did unto others as he would have them do unto him? Or a worshiper of the Crocodile God, who craves the honor of being thrown alive into the pit? Even the Samaritan, who started the whole thing...what made him think that the man he found lying at the roadside wanted to have oil poured in his wounds? What if the man was using those quiet moments to heal himself spiritually, enjoying the challenge of it?" I sounded convincing, to me.

"Even if the Rule was changed to *Do unto others as they want to be done to,* we can't know how anybody but ourselves wants to be done to. What the Rule means, and how we apply it honestly, is this: *Do unto others as you truly feel like doing unto others.* Meet a masochist with this rule and you do not have to flog him with his whip, simply because that is what he would want you to do unto him. Nor are you required to throw the worshiper to the crocodiles." I looked at him. "Too wordy?"

"As always. Richard, you are going to lose ninety percent of your audience unless you learn to *keep it short!*"

"Well, what's wrong with losing ninety percent of my audience?" I shot back at him. "What's wrong with losing ALL my audience? I know what I know and I talk what I talk! And if that's wrong then that's just too bad. The airplane rides are three dollars, cash!"

"You know what?" Shimoda stood up, brushing the hay off his blue jeans.

"What?" I said petulantly.

"You just graduated. How does it feel to be a Master?"

"Frustrating as hell."

He looked at me with an infinitesimal smile. "You get used to it," he said.

Here is
a test to find
whether your mission on earth
is finished: If you're alive,
it isn't.

16

Hardware stores are always long places, shelves going back into forever.

In Hayward Hardware I had gone hunting back in the dim, needing three-eighths-inch nuts and bolts and lockwashers for the tailskid of the Fleet. Shimoda browsed patiently as I looked, since of course he didn't need anything from a hardware store. The whole economy would collapse, I thought, if everybody was like him, making whatever they wanted out of thought-forms and thin air, repairing things without parts or labor.

At last I found the half-dozen bolts I needed and journeyed with them back toward the counter, where the owner had some soft music playing. *Greensleeves;* it was a melody that has haunted me happily since I was a boy, played now on a lute over some hidden sound system...strange to find in a town of four hundred souls.

Turned out it was strange for Hayward, too, for it wasn't a

sound system at all. The owner sat tilted back on his wooden stool at the counter, and listened to the messiah play the notes on a cheap six-string guitar from the sale shelf. It was a lovely sound, and I stood quiet there paying my seventy-three cents and being haunted again by the tune. Perhaps it was the tinny quality of the cheap instrument, but it still sounded far misty other-century England.

"Donald, that's beautiful! I didn't know you could play the guitar!"

"You didn't? Then you think somebody could have walked up to Jesus the Christ and handed him a guitar and he would have said, 'I can't play that thing'? Would he have said that?"

Shimoda put the guitar back in its place and walked out into the sunlight with me. "Or if somebody came by who spoke Russian or Persian, do you think any master worth his aura would not know what he was saying? Or if he wanted to skin a D-10 Cat or fly an airplane, that he couldn't do it?"

"So you really know all things, don't you?"

"You do too, of course. I just know that I know all things."

"I could play the guitar like that?"

"No, you'd have your own style, different from mine."

"How do I do that?" I wasn't going to run back and buy the guitar, I was just curious.

"Just give up all your inhibitions and all your beliefs that you can't play. Touch the thing as though it was a part of your life, which it is, in some alternate lifetime. Know that it's all right for you to play it well, and let your nonconscious self take over your fingers and play."

123

I had read something about that, hypnotic learning, where students were told they were masters of art, and so played and painted and wrote like master artists. "That's a hard thing, Don, to let go of my knowing that I can't play a guitar."

"Then it will be a hard thing for you to play the guitar. It will take years of practice before you give yourself permission to do it right, before your self-conscious mind tells you that you have suffered enough to have earned the right to play well."

"Why didn't it take me long to learn how to fly? That's supposed to be hard, but I picked it up pretty fast."

"Did you want to fly?"

"Nothing else mattered! More than anything! I was looking down on clouds, and the chimney-smoke in the mornings, going right straight up in the calm and I could see... Oh. I get your point. You're going to say, 'You never felt that way about guitars, did you?'"

"You never felt that way about guitars, did you?"

"And this sinking feeling I have right now, Don, tells me that is how you learned to fly. You just got into the Travel Air one day and you flew it. Never been up in an airplane before."

"My, you are intuitive."

"You didn't take the flying test for your license? No, wait. You don't even have a license, do you? A regular flying license."

He looked at me strangely, the whisper of a smile, as though I had dared him to come up with a license and he knew that he could do it.

"You mean the piece of paper, Richard? That kind of license?"

"Yes, the piece of paper."

He didn't reach into his pocket or bring out his wallet. He just opened his right hand and there was a flying license, as though he had been carrying it around, waiting for me to ask. It wasn't faded or bent, and I thought that ten seconds ago it hadn't existed at all.

But I took it and looked. It was an official pilot's certificate, Department of Transportation seal on it, *Donald William Shimoda*, with an Indiana address, licensed commercial pilot with ratings for single- and multi-engine land airplanes, instruments, and gliders.

"You don't have your seaplane ratings, or helicopter?"

"I'll have those if I need to have them," he said, so mysteriously that I burst out laughing before he did. The man sweeping the walk in front of the International Harvester place looked at us and smiled, too.

"What about me?" I said. "I want my airline transport rating."

"You're gonna have to forge your own licenses," he said.

17

ON THE Jeff Sykes radio talk show, I saw a Donald Shimoda I had never seen before. The show began at 9:00 p.m. and went till midnight, from a room no bigger than a watchmaker's, lined about with dials and knobs and racks of tape-cartridge commercial spots.

Sykes opened by asking if there wasn't something illegal about flying around the country in an ancient airplane, taking people for rides.

The answer is no, there is nothing illegal about it, the planes are inspected as carefully as any jet transport. They are safer and stronger than most sheet-metal modern airplanes, and all that's needed is a license and a farmer's permission. But Shimoda didn't say that. "No one can stop us from doing what we want to do, Jeff," he said.

Now that is quite true, but it had none of the tact that is called for when you are talking with a radio audience that is wondering what is going on, these airplanes flying around. A minute after he said that, the call-director telephone began lighting up on Sykes' desk.

"We have a caller on line one," Sykes said. "Go ahead, ma'am."

"Am I on the air?"

"Yes, ma'am, you are on the air and our guest is Mr. Donald Shimoda, the airplane flier. Go ahead, you are on the air."

"Well, I'd like to tell that fellow that not everybody gets to do what they want to do and that some people have to work for their living and hold down a little more responsibility than flying around with some carnival!"

"The people who work for a living are doing what they most want to do," Shimoda said. "Just as much as the people who play for a living..."

"Scripture says by the sweat of thy brow shalt thou earn thy bread, and in sorrow shalt thou eat of it."

"We're free to do that, too, if we want."

" 'Do your thing!' I get so tired of people like you saying do your thing, do your thing! You let everybody run wild, and they'll destroy the world. They are destroying the world right now. Look at what is happening to the green living things and the rivers and the oceans!"

She gave him fifty different openings to reply, and he ignored them all. "It's OK if the world is destroyed," he said. "There are a thousand million other worlds for us to create and choose from. As long as people want planets, there will be planets to live on."

That was hardly calculated to soothe the caller, and I looked at Shimoda, astonished. He was speaking from his viewpoint of perspectives over lots of lifetimes, learnings only a master can expect to recall. The caller was naturally assuming that the discussion had to do with the reality of this one world, birth is the beginning and death is the end. He knew that... why did he ignore it?

"Everything's OK, is it?" the caller said into her telephone. "There's no evil in this world, no sin going on all around us? That doesn't bother you, does it?"

"Nothing there to be bothered about, ma'am. We see just one little fleck of the whole that is life, and that one fleck is fake. Everything balances, and nobody suffers and nobody dies without their consent. Nobody does what they don't want to do. There is no good and there is no evil, outside of what makes us happy and what makes us unhappy."

None of it was making the lady on the phone any calmer. But she broke suddenly and said simply, "How do you know all these things that you say? How do you know what you say is true?"

"I don't know they're true," he said. "I believe them because it's fun to believe them."

I narrowed my eyes. He could have said that he had tried it and it works... the healings, the miracles, the practical living that made his thinking true and workable. But he didn't say that. Why?

There was a reason. I held my eyes barely open, most of the room gray, just a blurred fuzzy image of Shimoda leaning to talk into the microphone. He was saying all these things straight out, offering no choices, making no effort to help the poor listeners understand.

"Anybody who's ever mattered, anybody who's ever been happy, anybody who's ever given any gift into the world has been a divinely selfish soul, living for his own best interest. No exceptions."

It was a male caller next, while the evening fled by. "Selfish! Mister, do you know what the antichrist is?"

For a second Shimoda smiled and relaxed in his chair. It was as if he knew the caller personally.

"Perhaps you could tell me," he said.

"Christ said that we have to live for our fellow man. Antichrist says be selfish, live for yourself and let other people go to hell."

"Or heaven, or wherever else they feel like going."

"You are dangerous, do you know that, mister? What if everybody listened to you and did just whatever they felt like doing? What do you think would happen then?"

"I think that this would probably be the happiest planet in this part of the galaxy," he said.

"Mister, I am not sure that I want my children to hear what you are saying."

"What is it that your children want to hear?"

"If we are all free to do whatever we want to do, then I'm free to come out in that field with my shotgun and blow your fool head off."

"Of course you're free to do that."

There was a heavy click on the line. Somewhere in town there was at least one angry man. The others, and the angry women too, were on the telephone; every button on the machine was lit and flashing.

It didn't have to go that way; he could have said the same things differently and ruffled no feathers at all.

Sifting, sifting back over me was the same feeling I had in Troy, when the crowd broke and surrounded him. It was time, it was clearly time for us to be moving along.

The handbook was no help, there in the studio.

*In order
to live free and happily,
you must sacrifice
boredom. It is not always an easy
sacrifice.*

Jeff Sykes had told everybody who we were, that our airplanes were parked on John Thomas' hayfield on State 41, and that we slept nights under the wing.

I felt these waves of anger, from people frightened for their children's morality, and for the future of the American way of life, and none of it made me too happy. There was a half hour left of the show, and it only got worse.

130

"You know, mister, I think you're a fake," said the next caller.

"Of course I'm a fake! We're all fakes on this whole world, we're all pretending to be something that we're not. We are not bodies walking around, we are not atoms and molecules, we are unkillable undestroyable ideas of the Is, no matter how much we believe otherwise..."

He would have been the first to remind me that I was free to leave, if I didn't like what he was saying, and he would have laughed at my fears of lynch mobs waiting with torches at the airplanes.

18

*Don't be
dismayed at good-byes.
A farewell is necessary before
you can meet
again. And meeting
again, after moments or
lifetimes, is certain for
those who are
friends.*

NEXT NOON, before the people came to fly, he stopped by my wing. "Remember what you said when you found my problem, that nobody would listen, no matter how many miracles I did?"

"No."

"Do you remember that time, Richard?"

"Yeah, I remember the time. You looked so lonely, all of a sudden. I don't remember what I said."

"You said that depending on people to care about what I say is depending on somebody else for my happiness. That's what I came here to learn: *it doesn't matter whether I communicate or not*. I chose this whole lifetime to share with anybody the way the world is put together, and I might as well have chosen it to say nothing at all. The Is doesn't need me to tell anybody how it works."

"That's obvious, Don. I could have told you that."

"Thanks a lot. I find the one idea I lived this life to find, I finish a whole life's work, and he says, 'That's obvious, Don.' "

He was laughing, but he was sad, too, and at the time I couldn't tell why.

19

The mark
of your ignorance is the depth
of your belief in injustice
and tragedy. What the caterpillar
calls the end of the world,
the master calls a
butterfly.

T HE WORDS in the Handbook the day before were the only
warning I had. One second there was the normal little
crowd waiting to fly, his airplane taxiing in, stopping by them in a
whirl of propeller-wind, a casual good scene for me from the top
wing of the Fleet as I poured gas into the tank. The next second
there was a sound like a tire exploding and the crowd itself
exploded and ran. The tire on the Travel Air was untouched, the
engine ticked over at idle as it had a moment before, but there was a
foot-wide hole in the fabric under the pilot's cockpit and Shimoda
was pressed to the other side, head slammed down, his body still
as sudden death.

It took a few thousandths of a second for me to realize that Donald Shimoda had been shot, another to drop the gas can and jump off the top wing, running. It was like some movie script, some amateur-acted play, a man with a shotgun running away with everybody else, close enough by me I could have cut him with a sabre. I remember now that I didn't care about him. I was not enraged or shocked or horrified. The only thing that mattered was to get to the cockpit of the Travel Air as fast as I could and to talk with my friend.

It looked as if he had been hit by a bomb; the left half of his body was all torn leather and cloth and meat and blood, a soggy mass of scarlet.

His head was tilted down by the fuel primer knob, at the right lower corner of the instrument panel, and I thought that if he had been wearing his shoulder harness he wouldn't have been thrown forward like that.

"Don! Are you OK?" Fool's words.

He opened his eyes and smiled. His own blood was sprayed wet across his face. "Richard, what does it look like?"

I was enormously relieved to hear him talk. If he could talk, if he could think, he would be all right.

"Well, if I didn't know better, buddy, I'd say you had a bit of a problem."

He didn't move, except just his head a little bit, and suddenly I was scared again, more by his stillness than by the mess and the blood. "I didn't think you had enemies."

"I don't. That was . . . a friend. Better not to have . . . some hater bring all sorts of trouble . . . into his life . . . murdering me."

135

The seat and side panels of the cockpit were running with blood – it would be a big job just to get the Travel Air clean again, although the airplane itself wasn't damaged badly. "Did this have to happen, Don?"

"No..." he said faintly, barely breathing. "But I think...I like the drama..."

"Well, let's get cracking! Heal yourself! With the crowd that's coming, we got lots of flying to do!"

But as I was joking at him, and in spite of all his knowing and all his understanding of reality, my friend Donald Shimoda fell the last inch to the primer knob, and died.

There was a roaring in my ears, the world tilted, and I slid down the side of the torn fuselage into the wet red grass. It felt as if the weight of the Handbook in my pocket toppled me to my side, and as I hit the ground it fell loose, wind slowly ruffling the pages.

I picked it listlessly. Is this how it ends, I thought, is everything a master says just pretty words that can't save him from the first attack of some mad dog in a farmer's field?

I had to read three times before I could believe these were the words on the page.

*Everything
in this book
may be
wrong.*

⇜ end ⇝

Epilogue

B Y AUTUMN, I had flown south with the warm air. Good fields were few, but the crowds got bigger all the time. People had always liked to fly in the biplane, and these days more of them were staying to talk and to toast marshmallows over my campfire.

Once in a while somebody who hadn't really been much sick said they felt better for the talking, and the people next day would look at me strangely, move closer, curious. More than once I flew away early.

No miracles happened, although the Fleet was running better than ever she had, and on less gas. She had stopped throwing oil, stopped killing bugs on her propeller and windscreen. The colder air, no doubt, or the little fellas getting smart enough to dodge.

Still, one river of time had stopped for me that summer noon when Shimoda had been shot. It was an ending I could neither believe nor understand; it was stalled there and I lived it a thousand times again, hoping it might somehow change. It never did. What was I supposed to learn that day?

One night late in October, after I got scared and left a crowd in Mississippi, I came down in a little empty place just big enough to land the Fleet.

Once again before I slept, I thought back to that last moment – why did he die? There was no reason for it. If what he said was true...

There was no one now to talk with as we had talked, no one to learn from, no one to stalk and attack with my words, to sharpen my new bright mind against. Myself? Yes, but I wasn't half the fun that Shimoda had been, who taught by keeping me always off-balance with his spiritual karate.

Thinking this I slept, and sleeping, dreamed.

He was kneeling on the grass of a meadow, his back to me, patching the hole in the side of the Travel Air where the shotgun blast had been. There was a roll of Grade-A aircraft fabric and a can of butyrate dope by his knee.

I knew that I was dreaming, and I knew also that this was real. "DON!"

He stood slowly and turned to face me, smiling at my sorrow and my joy.

"Hi, fella," he said.

I couldn't see for tears. There is no dying, there is no dying at all, and this man was my friend.

"Donald!...*You're alive!* What are you trying to do?" I ran and threw my arms around him and he was real. I could feel the leather of his flying jacket, crush his arms inside it.

"Hi," he said. "Do you mind? What I am trying to do is to patch this hole, here."

I was so glad to see him, nothing was impossible.

"With the dope and fabric?" I said. "With dope and fabric you're trying to fix...? You don't do it that way, *you see it perfect,* already done..." and as I said the words I passed my hand like a screen in front of the ragged bloody hole and when my hand moved by, the hole was gone. There was just pure mirror-painted airplane left, seamless fabric from nose to tail.

"So that's how you do it!" he said, his dark eyes proud of the slow learner who made good at last as a mental mechanic.

I didn't find it strange; in the dream that was the way to do the job.

There was a morning fire by the wing, and a frying pan balanced over it. "You're cooking something, Don! You know, I've never seen you cook anything. What you got?"

"Pan-bread," he said matter-of-factly. "The one last thing I want to do in your life is show you how this is done."

He cut two pieces with his pocket knife and handed me one. The flavor is still with me as I write... the flavor of sawdust and old library paste, warmed in lard.

"What do you think?" he said.

"Don..."

141

"The Phantom's Revenge," he grinned at me. "I made it with plaster." He put his part back in the pan. "To remind you, if ever you want to move somebody to learn, do it with your knowing and not with your pan-bread, OK?"

"NO! Love me, love my pan-bread! It's the staff of life, Don!"

"Very well. But I guarantee – your first supper with anybody is going to be your last if you feed them that stuff."

We laughed and were quiet, and I looked at him in the silence.

"Don, you're all right, aren't you?"

"You expect me to be dead? Come now, Richard."

"And this is not a dream? I won't forget seeing you now?"

"No. This is a dream. It's a different space-time and any different space-time is a dream for a good sane earthling, which you are going to be for a while yet. But you will remember, and that will change your thinking and your life."

"Will I see you again? Are you coming back?"

"I don't think so. I want to get beyond times and spaces...I already am, as a matter of fact. But there is this link between us, between you and me and the others of our family. You get stopped by some problem, hold it in your head and go to sleep and we'll meet here by the airplane and talk about it, if you want."

"Don..."

"What?"

"Why the shotgun? Why did that happen? I don't see any power and glory in getting your heart blown out by a shotgun."

He sat down in the grass by the wing. "Since I was not a front-page Messiah, Richard, I didn't have to prove anything to anybody. And since you need the practice in being unflustered by